A

THOMAS BECON

AND

THE REFORMATION OF
THE CHURCH IN ENGLAND

VIVE MEMOR
LETHI

THOMAS BECONVS SACROSANCTÆ THEOLOGIÆ
PROFESSOR ANNO ÆTATIS SVÆ. 49. 1560.

Ora expressa vides, viuos imitantia vultus,
Quod potuit calimo, pictor, & arte vides.
Mentis quam nullus potuit tibi reddere pictor,
Effigiem scriptis, præbuit ipse suis.

THOMAS BECON

AND

THE REFORMATION
OF THE CHURCH
IN ENGLAND

DERRICK SHERWIN BAILEY, Ph.D.

CENTRAL LECTURER, CHURCH OF ENGLAND
MORAL WELFARE COUNCIL

OLIVER AND BOYD

EDINBURGH: TWEEDDALE COURT
LONDON: 98 GREAT RUSSELL STREET, W.C.

FIRST PUBLISHED   -   -   -   1952

PRINTED IN GREAT BRITAIN BY McCORQUODALE & CO., LTD.

TO

MY FATHER AND MOTHER

PREFACE

IN its original form this study was submitted as a thesis for the Doctorate of Philosophy (in Theology) at Edinburgh University. Publication has necessitated some drastic abbreviation, a very difficult operation for an author to perform successfully upon one of his own works ! I hope that the process of shortening in this case has been accomplished without in any way impairing the value of the book or leaving too obvious traces of the pruning to which it has been subjected. In particular it has meant that many quotations from Becon's works had to be curtailed or omitted, but I believe that the Parker Society edition is generally accessible, and as all the footnote references have been retained, it should not prove difficult to consult the passages themselves should the need arise.

I wish to express my gratitude to all who have so willingly assisted me in my researches, and first, to the Very Reverend Dr. Hugh Watt, sometime Principal of New College and Professor of Church History in the University of Edinburgh, for his interest, guidance and encouragement. I have also to thank Dr. Irene J. Churchill, F.S.A., Miss Lilian Redstone, M.B.E., and the Reverend J. F. Williams, M.A., F.S.A., Rector of South Walsham, for their valuable help and patient attention to my many letters of enquiry. I also wish to acknowledge with thanks the permission given by the Master and Fellows of Corpus Christi College, Cambridge, for the reproduction of the MS letter from Becon to Parker, now in the College Library. Finally, I must record my gratitude to the Carnegie Trust for a generous guarantee which has made publication possible.

D. S. B.

The Anglican Students' Chaplaincy,
Edinburgh,
September, 1950.

CONTENTS

PAGE

PREFACE - - - - - - - - - - vii

ABBREVIATIONS - - - - - - - - - xi

INTRODUCTION - - - - - - - - - xiii

CHAPTER

I EARLY YEARS AND UNIVERSITY LIFE, 1512-1531 - 1
II FROM ORDINATION TO FIRST RECANTATION, 1532-1541 - - - - - - - - 8
III RETIREMENT INTO KENT, 1541-1543 - - - 18
IV SECOND RECANTATION, 1543 - - - - 30
V WANDERINGS IN THE MIDLANDS, 1543-1547 - - 46
VI THE PROTESTANT ASCENDANCY, 1547-1553 - - 54
VII IMPRISONMENT AND EXILE, 1553-1558 - - - 77
VIII CANON OF CANTERBURY, 1559-1567 - - - 92
IX THOMAS BECON THE REFORMER - - - - 105
X THOMAS BECON THE WRITER - - - - 120
XI THE MAN AND HIS FAMILY - - - - - 124

DETACHED NOTES :

A. BIOGRAPHICAL MATERIAL - - - - - - 128
B. THE DATE OF THOMAS BECON'S BIRTH - - - 130
C. BECON'S ACADEMICAL CAREER - - - - - 131
D. BECON'S ORDINATION AND FIRST PREFERMENT - - 132
E. A SELECT COLLATION OF THE 1542 AND FOLIO EDITIONS OF THE *Potation for Lent* - - - 135
F. BECON'S *Catechism* - - - - - - 136

GENEALOGICAL TABLES :

1. THOMAS BECON'S FAMILY - - - - - - 138
2. INTER-RELATIONS OF DEDICATEES OF BECON'S WORKS 139

BIBLIOGRAPHIES :

I THOMAS BECON'S WORKS - - - - - - 140
II WORKS QUOTED OR MENTIONED - - - - 148

INDEX - - - - - - - - - - 152

ILLUSTRATIONS

THOMAS BECON : portrait from the folio edition of his works, 1560 - - - - - - - - *Frontispiece*

TITLE-PAGE OF *A New Pathway unto Prayer*, by ' Theodore Basille'. First edition, 1542 - - - - *Facing page* 20

THOMAS BECON IN 1553 : from the *Relics of Rome*, 1563 edition - - - - - - - - *Facing page* 77

FACSIMILE OF THOMAS BECON'S LETTER TO ARCHBISHOP PARKER - - - - - - - *Facing page* 104

ABBREVIATIONS

Ames, *Typ. Ant.* — Joseph Ames, *Typographical Antiquities*, ed. Dibdin.

Bale, *Catalogus* — John Bale, *Scriptorum Illustrium Maioris Britanniae Catalogus.*

Bale, *Index* — John Bale, *Index Britanniae Scriptorum*, ed. Poole and Bateson.

Bib. — Bibliography.

Burnet, *Reformation* — Gilbert Burnet, *History of the Reformation*, ed. N. Pocock.

Cooper, *Athenae* — C. H. and T. Cooper, *Athenae Cantabrigienses.*

DNB — *Dictionary of National Biography.*

Dixon, HCE — R. W. Dixon, *History of the Church of England.*

F — Thomas Becon's *Works*—Folio edition, 1560-64.

Foxe — John Foxe, *Acts and Monuments.*

Formularies — *Formularies of Faith, Henry VIII*, ed. Chas. Lloyd.

Garrett, *Exiles* — C. H. Garrett, *The Marian Exiles.*

Gee and Hardy, *Documents* — H. Gee and W. J. Hardy, *Documents Illustrative of English Church History.*

Hennessy, *Nov. Repert.* — G. Hennessy, *Novum Repertorium Ecclesiasticum Parochiale Londinense.*

L & P — *Letters and Papers.*

Le Neve, *Fasti* — J. le Neve, *Fasti Ecclesiae Anglicanae.*

Newcourt, *Repertorium* — R. Newcourt, *Repertorium Ecclesiasticum Parochiale Londonense.*

Orig. Let. — *Original Letters relative to the English Reformation*, ed. Hastings Robinson, Parker Society.

P	Thomas Becon's *Works*—Parker Society edition.
PS	Parker Society.
STC	*Short Title Catalogue of English Books*, 1475-1640, Pollard and Redgrave.
Strype, *Annals*	John Strype, *Annals of the Reformation*.
Strype, *Aylmer*	John Strype, *Life and Acts of John Aylmer*.
Strype, *Cranmer*	John Strype, *Memorials of Thomas Cranmer*.
Strype, *Eccl. Mem.*	John Strype, *Ecclesiastical Memorials*.
Strype, *Grindal*	John Strype, *History of the Life and Acts of Edmund Grindal*.
Strype, *Parker*	John Strype, *Life and Acts of Matthew Parker*.
Tanner	Thomas Tanner, *Bibliotheca Britannico-Hibernia*.
Troubles	*A Brieff discours off the troubles begonne at Franckford* (1845 reprint of 1575 Black Letter edition).
Venn, *Alumni*	J. Venn, *Alumni Cantabrigienses*.

INTRODUCTION

FEW contemporary verdicts have been more completely reversed than that passed by his fellow reformers and protestant countrymen upon Thomas Becon. From the scant mention which his life and works now receive at the hands of historians it would hardly be inferred that he was a prolific and influential religious propagandist, some of whose tracts were for many years " best-sellers " ; a popular preacher whose vigorous sermons were greatly esteemed by those of his own persuasion ; and a zealous supporter of the Reformation in England. It is true that he never appears as one of the principal actors in the dramatic events of his time (though there are, I believe, good reasons for this), and that in the end, although marked down for high preferment, he was passed over, while many with whom he had borne the rigours of persecution and imprisonment and the hardships of exile were rewarded with deaneries and bishoprics. Nevertheless, he was no less active and influential in the religious struggle than they, and the concern with which opponents of the Reformation regarded his writings, while no indication of their intrinsic merit, is at least ample testimony to their vogue and power. The oblivion into which he has fallen contrasts strangely with his former prominence. He has joined that numerous company of his contemporaries whose names catch the eye as we turn the pages of Foxe or Strype—those men of whose lives and thought and contribution to the success or failure of the great movements of their time we know little or nothing.

It would not, of course, be difficult to find reasons for the neglect of one who never became a conspicuous figure among the English Reformers. It cannot be denied, for instance, that Becon's writing, though once highly esteemed and certainly not lacking in freshness, vigour and a Latimer-like homeliness, is not generally distinguished by great originality or depth of theological perception. To look for such qualities is to miss his real importance. Becon excelled as a popular and able exponent of Reformation teaching who knew (sometimes only too well) how to attract and hold the attention of the ordinary reader. He was a propagandist—a vociferous shouter of slogans and battle-cries who could kindle the enthusiasm which others were able to turn to account. He appealed to the emotions rather than to the intellect. His ability did not lie conspicuously in the elaboration of a reasoned apologetic (he was usually content with simple assertions), but few of his contemporaries surpassed him in the abusive, coarse and sometimes grossly vulgar polemic which was so congenial to the taste of the sixteenth century. Although his fame rested in part upon his devotional works, these do not stand in the mainstream of Christian tradition, and often reflect the intense but narrow piety of an incipient Puritanism. He was, in short, essentially the kind of man to make his mark during critical and troubled times, when party feeling ran high ; one likely both to be appreciated and even over-valued by his contemporaries, and to be forgotten by their descendants, to whom he left no notable and permanent legacy either as constructive theologian or as ecclesiastical statesman, and not even a memory of great deeds wrought or great sufferings undergone.

But when every allowance has been made, the neglect into which Thomas Becon has been permitted to fall still remains undeserved and regrettable, and to attempt to redress the balance is no mere antiquarian labour. He has a claim upon our attention as a vigorous, effective and influential protagonist of the protestant cause, as a typical English reformed church-man of the period, and as a colourful personality in whose life and works the course and character of the English Reformation are mirrored. It is the aim of this study to try to rescue his name from its unmerited oblivion, and to give some account of the part which he played in the reformation of the Church in England.

Not least among the difficulties with which the biographer of Thomas Becon has to contend are the elusiveness of his subject and the paucity of the material at his disposal. The latter[1] is not only meagre (which may partly account for the neglect Becon has suffered) but often confused or inaccurate.

[1] See Detached Note A.

He was reticent, perhaps advisedly, about his activities at certain periods ; he tells us little of his early life ; he is silent upon family matters (apart from mentioning the names of his children) ; and, so far as I can ascertain, made no will. To the comparatively few facts which can be gleaned from his writings, official and other contemporary records add but little, and several periods of his life are particularly obscure. Although frequently involved in important events, he seems to have remained in the background ; hence, as in the case of the Frankfort " troubles ", his precise views and actions cannot always be ascertained. Allowance has to be made for the partiality and anti-catholic prejudices of certain early memoir writers and historians. Finally, the many different spellings of Becon's name cause confusion, which is increased by his adoption of the pseudonym Theodore Basil[le] during Henry VIII's reign. Some biographers have added to the confusion by mistaking him for a younger contemporary, John Becon of St. John's College, Cambridge, who became Chancellor of Norwich.

This study has afforded an opportunity to correct many of the errors which have thus arisen, and to present for the first time information which throws new light upon Becon's life. In addition, much material already accessible in printed records, but hitherto unused, has been included. Since they are now little known, I have quoted somewhat freely from his works. Citations, wherever possible, are from the Parker Society edition, to which references have also been made, as it is not difficult to come by ; for works not included in that edition, the rare folio or another early edition has been used.[1] When compelled by lack of data I have not hesitated to suggest what has seemed to me, after careful consideration, the most probable course of events ; such reconstructions serve to bridge the many gaps in the story of Becon's life, and I hope in every case that it will be quite clear what is fact and what conjecture. I have tried, and I trust successfully, to avoid writing yet another account of the English Reformation, and have confined myself simply to the events and ideas which are reflected in Becon's life and works.

[1] In footnote references the Parker Society edition is designated P, and the folio edition F.

CHAPTER I

EARLY YEARS AND UNIVERSITY LIFE
1512-1531

W E do not know the exact date of Thomas Becon's birth, but there is good reason for thinking that it occurred sometime during the year beginning 25th March, 1512 (old style).[1] An allusion to sheepfarming practice in "my country of Norfolk "[2] suggests that his home was on the west side of that county, where sheep then abounded, but it cannot be more precisely located. Little is known about his parents and their circumstances. His father probably died while Becon was still young, for his mother, who had married again, lost her second husband in 1546.[3] It seems unlikely that Becon came of an influential or well-to-do family. He appears to have depended for advancement upon his writings and upon the active and enthusiastic support of the Reformation which commended him to his patrons, and the shadow of poverty which overclouded much of his life suggests that he inherited no wealth or property. He never mentions brothers or sisters, and his being summoned home on the death of his step-father to be the " staff " of his mother's old age[4] may mean that he was an only child. His younger contemporary, John Becon, may have been a relative.

[1] See Detached Note B.
[2] P i, p. 9 ; cf Bale, *Catalogus*, p. 756 (" patria Nordovolgius ") ; also an allusion by Becon in *The Fortress of the Faithful*, P ii, p. 596. Strype, *Aylmer*, p. 5, has Norfolk, but in *Cranmer*, i, p. 607, followed by Brook, *Lives of the Puritans*, i, p. 166, and by others also, he gives Becon's county as Suffolk, due probably to confusion with John Becon, who was born there (Venn, *Alumni*, I, i, p. 114). The dedication of the *Commonplaces of the Holy Scriptures* to " my dear countrymen and faithful ministers of the Gospel of Jesu Christ, watching and attending upon the Lord's flock in the parishes of Norfolk and Suffolk " (P iii, p. 290) is explained by the fact that the Norwich diocese then embraced both counties.
[3] *The Jewel of Joy*, P ii, p. 426.
[4] ibid.

I

Becon's early life was probably passed amid humble surroundings in a quiet west-Norfolk village. It is not difficult to imagine how much his developed religious opinions may have owed to impressions received during boyhood, for he belonged to the social stratum in which Lollardism had principally survived, and he may well have heard from time to time among his elders the surreptitious talk which occasionally blazed up into open and fanatical preaching of communism and anticlericalism.[1] Before he was ten years old, too, Lutheran opinions had begun to circulate in England. To the coast towns of East Anglia the vessels of the Hanse traders brought the books of the Reformer and news of the events in Germany, and sympathizers sprang up everywhere in Norfolk and Suffolk. The young boy would soon learn something of the excitement and its cause, and on the eve of his departure to Cambridge he may have been among those who thronged to hear Thomas Bilney during his preaching tour in the spring of 1526-27. Although Becon says nothing about these early years, and acknowledges no formative influences, it was perhaps not without good reason that at the University he found Latimer's preaching congenial, and became so assiduous a hearer and student of his sermons.[2]

II

Thomas Becon probably entered Cambridge in March, 1526-27.[3] It is generally stated that he was a member of St. John's College,[4] but the authority for this cannot be discovered, and it must remain no more than a reasonable assumption.[5]

[1] At the beginning of the sixteenth century, especially in the Norwich diocese, there seems to have been a revival of Lollardism—" heresy " then could hardly denote anything else : see Foxe, iv, pp. 126, 174, 180-181, 214-216, 773 ; v, pp. 647 and 652.

[2] The Jewel of Joy, P ii, p. 424.

[3] See Detached Note B.

[4] Ayre, Preface P i, p. vii ; Cooper, Athenae, i, p. 246 ; Venn, Alumni, I, i, p. 114.

[5] Excluding Thomas, Venn lists ten Becons or Beacons, of whom four were members of St. John's College, including Thomas's son Theodore. This may perhaps account for the assumption that Thomas himself was also a member of that College.

The reforming movement at Cambridge of which Erasmus was the precursor and Bilney the initiator had by this time taken on a pronouncedly Lutheran colouring. Its acknowledged leader was Latimer, and the young Becon, " a poor scholar . . . very desirous to have the knowledge of good letters "[1] and " studious of the holy scripture " from his youth,[2] went frequently to hear him preach. So great was Latimer's influence that Becon declares :

> . . . to [him] next unto God I am specially bound to give most hearty thanks for the knowledge, if any I have, of God and of his most blessed word.

He gives a vivid description of Latimer's preaching and its effect, but his accuracy in one respect has been challenged. He says :

> I was present when, with manifest authorities of God's word and arguments invincible, besides the allegations of doctors, he proved in his sermons, that the holy scriptures ought to be read in the English tongue of all christian people, whether they were priests or laymen, as they be called . . .

Wharton asserts that Latimer, so far from maintaining this doctrine, joined with the bishops and others in condemning the circulation of the scriptures in the vernacular by signing the proclamation issued after the conference at Westminster Palace in May, 1530.[3] This, however, is clearly a misrepresentation. Latimer's name was certainly appended to the proclamation, with the names of the others who had taken part in the deliberations, but there is nothing to show that this was done by his wish, or that he approved of the decision reached. His consistent demand for a Bible in the common tongue, and the bold appeal which he addressed not long after to Henry VIII urging him to expedite the preparation of the promised authorized version, are sufficient to vindicate Latimer. But there seems to be no record of his preaching in favour of the

[1] *The Jewel of Joy*, P ii, p. 424. Becon's account of his life at Cambridge (pp. 424-426) is put into the mouth of *Christopher* and not into that of *Philemon*, who usually represents him in the dialogues, but there is no doubt that Becon's own experiences and views are recorded.

[2] *The New Year's Gift*, P i, p. 309, from where Bale's statement, " professione theologus ab ipsa adolescentia " (*Catalogus*, p. 756) is apparently taken.

[3] See Wharton's " Observations " upon the *Memorials* in Strype, *Cranmer*, ii, pp. 1058-1059.

English Bible, though Foxe says that he did so in one of the
" Card " sermons which is not now extant.[1] It would have
been strange, however, had he not alluded to the subject from
a Cambridge pulpit, and there seems no reason to doubt
the accuracy of Becon's memory.

He is less reliable, however, in his reference to the second
of the surviving " Card " sermons :

> Neither was I absent when he inveighed against temple-works,
> good intents, blind zeal, superstitious devotion, etc.; as the
> painting of tabernacles, gilding of images, setting up of candles,
> running on pilgrimages, and such other idle inventions of men,[2]
> whereby the glory of God was obscured, and the works of mercy
> the less regarded.

Perhaps from forgetfulness, but more probably for polemical
reasons, Becon fails to make clear Latimer's precise position at
this time :

> No doubt the voluntary works be good and ought to be done ;
> but yet they must be so done, that by their occasion the necessary
> works and the works of mercy be not decayed and forgotten.[3]

Latimer never condemned the doing of voluntary works
supplementary to those of mercy or necessity, but only the
doctrine of merit attached by the medieval Church to such
works, and the tendency in consequence to regard them as the
easier way of earning merit.[4]

It seems likely that the young student was on intimate
terms with the preacher whom he so much admired. The
tribute which he pays to Latimer's influence suggests this, and
it may be with grateful recollection of assistance of a more
material kind that he records

---

[1] Foxe, vii, p. 438.

[2] *cf* Latimer's list of " will-works," as Becon calls them : ". . . to build
churches, to give ornaments to God and his altar, to gild saints . . .", *Sermons*
(PS), p. 22 ; " setting up candles, gilding and painting, building of churches,
giving of ornaments, going on pilgrimages, making of highways . . .", ibid,
p. 23.

[3] ibid, p. 23 ; *cf* Latimer's first Sermon to the Convocation of 1536,
Sermons (PS), p. 37 ; his episcopal Injunctions of 1537, *Remains* (PS), p. 243 ;
and a letter to Warham, ibid, p. 353, where his position is clearly stated.

[4] The " Card " sermons aroused the hostility of Latimer's opponents, and
Buckenham, Prior of the Dominicans, attempted a rejoinder which fell rather
flat. Becon may be alluding to the Prior and his supporters when he writes
of ". . . divers drowsy duncers, with certain false flying flattering friars " who
" openly in their unsavoury sermons resisted [Latimer's] godly purpose . . .",
i.e., his advocacy of the vernacular Bible.

. . . how beneficial he was, according to his possibility, to poor scholars and other needy people.

Quoting a proverb current in the University many years after : " When Master Stafford read, and Master Latimer preached, then was Cambridge blessed", Becon in his account proceeds to some reminiscences of George Stafford. He describes him as

> . . . a man of a very perfect life, and (if I may so speak) of an angelic conversation, approvedly learned in the Hebrew, Greek, and Latin tongues, and such one as had, through his painful labours, obtained singular knowledge in the mysteries of God's most blessed word.

He seems to have attended the lectures which Stafford delivered as Lady Margaret Reader in Divinity, and writes of them thus :

> . . . as he beautified the letters of blessed Paul with his godly expositions,[1] so likewise did he learnedly set forth in his lectures the native sense and true understanding of the four evangelists, vively restoring unto us the apostle's mind, and the mind of those holy writers, which so many years before had lien unknown and obscured through the darkness and mists of the Pharisees and papists.

In this mood of enthusiastic recollection he even doubts whether Stafford was more bound to St. Paul for his " godly epistles," or the Apostle to his expositor for setting forth their meaning plainly and simply, untrammelled by

> . . . the foolish fantasies and elvish expositions of certain doting doctors, and, as it were, drowned in the dirty dregs of the drowsy duncers.[2]

Unfortunately Becon is so preoccupied with his panegyric upon Latimer and Stafford that he tells us nothing of his own life at Cambridge, and does not refer to events such as the question of the King's divorce, though Cranmer's treatise on the lawfulness of marriage with a brother's wife, and the University's decision in the matter, must have caused considerable stir among junior as well as among senior members of the Colleges. But four such impressionable years spent in Cambridge during the time that the University was the scene of the first serious clashes between the reformers and their

---

[1] Latimer gives a specimen of Stafford's exposition in the seventh *Sermon on the Lord's Prayer*, *Sermons* (PS), pp. 440-441.
[2] duncers=followers of Duns Scotus.

conservative opponents cannot have been without great and lasting influence. With whatever views Becon entered Cambridge, his remarks in *The Jewel of Joy* show that his character and opinions were largely formed by those whom he met, and by the events in which he, with his fellow students, must have taken a deep and often violently partisan interest.

Among Becon's contemporaries were some who must have had congenial views, and with several of whom he was closely associated in after years. Anthony Gilby and Richard Alvey were both exiles at Frankfort during Mary's reign ; John Cheke, before he was captured and apostasized, had settled at Strasbourg during the exile ; Thomas Bernard was later, like Becon, a chaplain to Cranmer ; and William Turner was appointed physician and chaplain to the Duke of Somerset. Turner had as patron Thomas, Lord Wentworth, who later interested himself in Becon also, and to Turner's *Preservative or Triacle against the poison of Pelagius* Becon appended a Latin commendatory poem. Nor must we omit to mention a close friend of later years who may have been studying at Cambridge during this time—Robert Wisdom. Among the more senior men were John Bale, afterwards Bishop of Ossory and an exile, who ended his days with Becon as a fellow canon at Canterbury, and John Ponet, in 1532 fellow of Queens', who became Bishop of Winchester and on Mary's accession sought safety, like Becon, in Strasbourg.

We do not know whether, under such influences, Becon immediately embraced the cause of the reformers, or whether the seed was being sown which was later to bear fruit. But we can hardly doubt that all his sympathies and interests were set in a protestant direction from the first, and it was not long before he attracted attention as one of those who were favourably disposed towards the Reformation.

Becon was admitted a bachelor of arts in 1530-31,[1] probably completing his *stans in quadragesima*[2] early in April, 1531. We do not know why he did not then proceed to his master's degree,[3] nor do we know whether he left the University

[1] Cooper, *Athenae*, i, p. 246 ; Venn, *Alumni*, I, i, p. 114.
[2] See J. B. Mullinger, *The University of Cambridge*, i, pp. 352-355.
[3] On the question of Becon's subsequent academic career, see Detached Note C.

forthwith, or remained there for the rest of the year. He may have returned home, or have been occupied with making arrangements for the future ; or he may immediately have entered the College of St. John the Evangelist, Rushworth, as a probationer, for in 1532 he is found in residence there, and in July of that year was admitted a member of the community.

CHAPTER II

FROM ORDINATION TO FIRST RECANTATION
1532-1541

I

ON the strength of a statement in the preface to the folio edition of Becon's works,[1] dated 17th January, 1564,[2] it has been assumed without question that he was ordained in 1538 or thereabout. Further, it is generally supposed that he was almost immediately preferred to the vicarage of Brenzett in Kent.[3] For neither of these alleged facts, however, can the least shred of substantiating evidence be discovered. The matter is fully discussed in Detached Note D, and need not detain us here, for in the Norwich Episcopal Register there are four entries, hitherto unpublished, which finally settle the point. They relate to ordinations by John Underwood, a suffragan of Norwich and titular Bishop of Chalcedon :

> 25th May, 1532, Thomas Becon of Norwich diocese ordained exorcist and acolyte.
> 13th March, 1532-3, Thomas Becon, *secularis*, of Norwich diocese, ordained sub-deacon to the title of the College of St. John the Evangelist, Rushworth, in the Lady Chapel.
> 29th March, 1533, Thomas Becon, *secularis*, ordained deacon. [The same title and place.]
> 12th April, 1533, Thomas Becon, *secularis*, ordained priest. [The same title and place.]

There is no doubt that these entries refer to the subject of this study, who, as already suggested, may have entered the College as a probationer soon after leaving Cambridge.

[1] P i, p. 27 : " I . . . have done mine endeavour these twenty-six years (so long have I travailed in the ministry) both by preaching and writing . . ."
[2] In this case, apparently, 1563-4 ; Becon had probably adopted during his exile the Continental style of reckoning the year from 1st January.
[3] Tanner, p. 85, followed in all subsequent biographical notices.

II

Rushworth (the name was changed to Rushford in the seventeenth century) lies on the southern boundary of Norfolk about four miles east of Thetford. There, in 1342, Edmund Gonvile, Rector of Rushworth, founded the College of St. John the Evangelist. It was intended to be an experiment in a new kind of community life. The great monastic houses, absorbing lands and benefices in their encroachments, had so increased in wealth and power as to become in some measure independent of royal and episcopal authority alike. Inevitably there followed a lowering of standards and the decay of spiritual religion, not to mention the gradual exclusion of lay influence from the Church. The mendicant orders, which had brought about a temporary revival and had gained the support of the people, fell victims in their turn to the laxity and secularity which are the attendant dangers of success. Gonvile saw that something different was needed :

. . . a college, or simple community, of priests living together in God's service, under the direct control of the Bishop of the diocese, holding their property on condition of strict obedience to statutes and regulations ordained by their founder, and subject at every point of their conduct to the Bishop's visitation and authority.[1]

With this ideal in mind, he fitted out an ancient moated manor house, with an old chapel attached, so as to accommodate a Master and four Fellows, and endowed the College with the Rectory of Rushworth. The foundation was at first purely religious. The Master had the general oversight of the house and pastoral charge of the parish of Rushworth ; the Fellows, each in his turn, saw to the due performance of the chapel services.[2] Near the end of the fifteenth century the College

---

[1] E. K. Bennet, *The College of St. John the Evangelist of Rushworth*, in *Norfolk Archaeology*, vol. x, pt. iii, p. 291. This article gives a complete account of the College.

[2] Every day special prayers were offered by the College in chapter for the founder and all benefactors, and the Mattins of St. Mary, the Mattins and Hours of the day, and four Masses, were said, and in addition the Placebo and the Dirige were recited publicly in chapel. No provision was made for Vespers, Compline, or other offices. The founder's anniversary was observed " solemnly " by the whole College ; see another article by Dr. Bennet in *Norfolk Archaeology*, vol. x, pt. i, pp. 50-64.

benefited from an endowment by Lady Anne Wingfield for the erection and maintenance of a Grammar School for thirteen children of the Norwich diocese, of whom five were to be fed, clothed, and brought up within the College, while the other eight received their education free. Two " honest priests", designated " Dame Anny's priests", were added to the establishment ; they had to be born in the diocese, and were required to say daily masses and orisons with special suffrages for the foundress and other benefactors. Moreover, one always had to be

> . . . well studyd and lernyd in grammer abyll to teche grammer and usually techyng alle convenient tymes grammer in Russhe-worthe aforeseid to the said v childeryn and to other viij poore childeryn, noothing takyng for that hys labor or attendance bewaye of salarye or scole lier for or of any of the same xiij childeryn.

The actual strength of the College establishment is not easy to ascertain. A letter from the Bishop, written soon after the date of foundation, refers to seven secular priests, possibly because two chaplains attached to a chantry founded by Gonvile had been incorporated into the College. The five boarding scholars were intended to correspond to five Fellows, but Dugdale specifies a Master or Warden and six secular priests,[1] by which he may mean either six Fellows, or the four Fellows of the original foundation and the two " Dame Anny's priests".

At the end of the fifteenth century Rushworth was a prosperous college, but thereafter a decline set in ; the number of scholars diminished and they were allowed to go sheep-watching instead of attending to their studies, the statutes were ignored and not read publicly, and fellowships were left vacant.[2] There were, however, no grave scandals at Rushworth, but simply slovenliness and lack of discipline. In this respect the College, even in its decadence, contrasted favourably with many of the greater religious houses, and the reasons are not far to seek. It had no great endowments or extensive

---

[1] *Monasticon*, vi, p. 1385.
[2] Compare the visitation of 23rd June, 1514, with those of 23rd June, 1520, and 20th July, 1526—see A. Jessop, *Visitations of the Diocese of Norwich*, pp. 91, 156, and 244-245.

properties; it lacked the influence which might have encouraged interference in ecclesiastical politics ; its Master and Fellows were seculars, subject to control and visitation by the diocesan, and almost certainly men of no great social consequence and unlikely to be connected with any of the great families ; and, not least, the difference in ideals, tradition, and function must have counted for something.

III

We do not know what attracted Becon to this venerable community,[1] but his object in joining it was clearly to under-take the instruction of the boys. This suggests that in the educational work at least a revival was beginning to take place at the College ; certainly at the next sexennial visitation on 18th July, 1532, less than two months after Becon's ordination as exorcist and acolyte, there were no complaints about the depletion of the number of scholars. On this occasion the business was simply routine. George Wyndham, the Master, was absent, but Thomas Barnesdale, Robert Locke, William Fisher, and John Croftes, the senior Fellows, were there. With them was Edward Hanson, another Fellow who had not been sworn, and now took the oath. Thomas Becon himself, " artium baccalaurius, acolitus, praeceptor puerorum", and Thomas Horne, were admitted Fellows of the College.

It appears from the transactions at this visitation that although his work was to teach the boys, Becon was not one of the two chaplains mentioned in the Lady Anne's bequest ; indeed, not being in priest's orders, he was not at that time qualified for the position. In the injunctions issued at the visitation the chaplains' duties are stated to be the saying of mass for the soul of their benefactress, and nothing is said about the original stipulation that one of them must be qualified to teach. It seems probable that the tutorial chaplain had been relieved of his scholastic duties and restricted, like his fellow chaplain, to altar services alone. His work had then been

---

[1] It is possible that Becon's home was near Rushworth ; had he been at one time a foundation scholar ? Unfortunately no records of the " childeryn " have survived.

delegated to a qualified instructor, and Becon had been appointed specially to teach the boys grammar.[1]

He remained at Rushworth for at least a further nine months, but after his ordination to the priesthood on 12th April, 1533, all trace of him is lost for more than five years. His name does not appear among those of the " Magister et confratres Collegii de Rushworth " who, " uno ore ", signified their acknowledgment of the royal supremacy on 25th August, 1534.[2] As the submission seems to have been unanimous it is probable that of those enumerated in the visitation record of 1532, both Becon and Edward Hanson had left the College. The Norwich registers contain no entry respecting the presentation of Becon to any benefice within the diocese,[3] and it is probable that after relinquishing his appointment at Rushworth he continued his work as a teacher in the house of some gentleman.

IV

Thomas Becon's name next occurs in connexion with the chantry of St. Thomas the Martyr in the church of St. Lawrence, Ipswich.[4] The chantry was founded in 1514 by Edmund Daundy, a merchant of the town, who appointed James Crawford to serve it. At the time of the rebellions of 1536 Crawford attracted attention, probably by giving utterance to some incautious expression of sympathy with the insurgents or their cause.[5] He was indicted for treason, but for some reason no proceedings were taken against him. Two years later, however, the charge was renewed, and the bailiffs of Ipswich reported the matter to Cromwell on 15th December, 1538.[6]

[1] Becon seems to have been the only member of the community to possess a degree ; none of the others is shown as having any qualification.

[2] *Norfolk Archaeology*, vol. x, pt. iii, p. 373 ; the signatories, in order, are : Wyndham (the Master), Barnesdale, Locke, Croftes, Fisher, and Horne.

[3] It should be noted that the episcopal registers are somewhat mutilated. Several of the pages for 1535 are torn and entries are missing, while the pages for the period August, 1535, to March, 1536, have entirely disappeared. It is always possible that a reference to Becon occurred, which can no longer be traced.

[4] For a description of this foundation, with a transcript of Daundy's will, see J. Wodderspoon, *Memorials of Ipswich*, pp. 348-353.

[5] *cf* an incident mentioned by Dixon, HCE, i, p. 487.

[6] L & P Henry VIII, xi, No. 1309, p. 530—an entry which has been incorrectly calendared, and relates to 1538.

On the same day Thomas, Lord Wentworth of Nettlestead, also wrote to the Vicar General in support of the bailiffs and the parishioners of St. Lawrence's. Unfortunately his letter is ambiguous :

> At the time of the last insurrection in the North parts, the then bailiffs reported his [Crawford's] demeanour to me, which accords with the certificate they have made to your Lordship. They deprived him of the chantry because he did not keep the ordinances made by . . . Edmond Daundy, and have at my request appointed Thomas Bekone, a discreet, honest priest, well learned, a true preacher of the Word of God, a great setter forth to the people of the King's most just and lawful title of supremacy, approved by God's word.[1]

It is not clear whether the " certificate " was the bailiffs' letter of 15th December, 1538, or a report of the original indictment of 1536 ; nor whether the deprivation of Crawford was the act of the bailiffs in office in the latter year,[2] or of those who advised Cromwell of the renewal of the treason charge.[3] Despite the vagueness of his language, however, I think we can assume that Wentworth refers to events which happened in December, 1538.

Wentworth's letter shows that since leaving Rushworth Becon had become known as a serviceable supporter of the Reformation, and his appointment was probably intended to counteract Crawford's reactionary teaching. Cromwell would understand by " discreet " and " honest " that Becon was circumspect yet reliable as an advocate of the protestant cause, and his assiduity in preaching the royal supremacy would further recommend him to the Vicar General, who for more than three years had been directing against the monasteries the power of the Supreme Head.

Concerning the appointment itself there is some mystery, for it does not appear that Becon took up his duties as priest of St. Thomas's chantry. His name does not occur in the records of the Corporation of Ipswich, but Crawford, on the other hand, seems to have remained in the town, for he witnessed wills on 4th July, 1539, 13th December, 1540, and

---

[1] L & P Henry VIII, xiii, pt. ii, No. 1063, p. 453.
[2] Robert Daundy (who brought up the treason charge again in 1538) and John Butler.
[3] Nicholas Hervy and Rauf Goodwyn.

20th December, 1540, describing himself in the last case as
" chantry priest of St. Lawrence."[1] Becon may have declined
the preferment, but there is also the possibility that by
intruding him Wentworth and the bailiffs aroused unexpected
opposition. The fact that Crawford remained in Ipswich and
seems to have resumed his duties suggests that he was not
without strong support, and there is something suspicious about
his being deprived for non-observance of the ordinances of the
founder, while under indictment for treason. We do not know
what local animosities and intrigues underlay the whole
incident, but whatever the reason, Thomas Becon did not
become Edmund Daundy's priest, and once again, this time for
nearly three years, we lose all trace of his movements.

Wentworth's interest in Becon was probably due to the
fact that the young priest was known and befriended by people
who were likely to be familiar to the Lord of Nettlestead.
Becon's *Invective against Swearing*, for instance, is dedicated to
Richard Scott, whose mother was the only daughter of Reginald
Pimpe of Nettlestead, and Wentworth's third son, Richard,
married a Margaret Roydon who may well have been the sister
or daughter of Thomas Roydon, to whom the *New Year's Gift*
is inscribed, and who married Margaret Whetnall, the aunt of
Scott's wife, Mary.[2] It seems probable that Becon had many
well-wishers among these and other families which were united
by ties of marriage and of sympathy with the Reformation,
and that he first attracted Wentworth's notice as a private
tutor or chaplain in the service of one of them.

V

Becon was not one of the first to experience the rigour of
the anti-protestant statute of the Six Articles, which came into
force on 12th July, 1539, but eventually he fell foul of the

[1] *Register of Wills and Deeds*, foll. 42, 27, and 25. In 1546 the chantry
priest was Thomas Pecocke—*Chantry Certificates, Suffolk*, 1546, return 45,
entry 34, at the Public Record Office ; see V. B. Redstone, *Chapels, Chantries,
and Gilds in Suffolk* in *Suff. Inst. of Archaeology and Nat. Hist.*, xii (1), 1904.

[2] For these family connexions, see Genealogical Table 2.

authorities. On 29th January, 1540-41, a commission " for
heresies and other offences " in the city and diocese of London
was set up under Bonner. Some two hundred were accused,
but all except three were pardoned and discharged.[1] Foxe
gives a catalogue of the " heretics " concerned, and their
offences, in which this entry occurs :

> The same time also Robert Wisedom, parish priest of St.
> Margaret's in Lothbury, and Thomas Becon, were brought to
> Paul's Cross, to recant and to revoke their doctrine, and to burn
> their books.[2]

Hence it has generally been assumed that Becon and his friend
were among those brought before the commission,[3] but the
evidence needs re-examination.

The two hundred against whom proceedings were taken
seem to have been released almost immediately, and the whole
business was probably concluded before the end of March,
1540-41. Wisdom, however, according to his own account,[4]
was not apprehended until Sunday, 17th July, 1541 ; he was
examined that afternoon, and made his submission on the
following day, after which he was released with the assurance
that no further reference would be made to the matter. He
says nothing about a recantation or the burning of his books,
and this was certainly not the occasion, as some have asserted,[5]
when he was committed to the Lollards' Tower.[6] It is clear
that Foxe, never the most accurate of historians, did not know
when Wisdom was charged, and simply assumed that he was
among those presented in January and February.

---

[1] For an account of the proceedings, see Foxe, v, pp. 440-451 ; Strype,
Eccl. Mem., I, i, pp. 565-567.

[2] Foxe, v, p. 448.

[3] See, e.g., Strype, *Eccl. Mem.*, I, i, p. 567 ; Dixon, HCE, ii, p. 269, &c.

[4] See Foxe, v, App. XXII*.

[5] Strype, *Eccl. Mem.*, I, i, p. 570, followed by Cooper, *Athenae*, i, p. 260,
Garrett, *Exiles*, p. 340, and others.

[6] Wisdom's refutation of the thirteen articles alleged against him at the
time of his imprisonment in the Lollards' Tower (see Strype, *Eccl. Mem.*,
I, ii, pp. 463-479) makes it clear that this imprisonment occurred just before
his recantation in 1543. Due to this confusion of dates, Strype says that
Wisdom had been " in trouble before the Bishop of London " in 1538 (*Eccl.
Mem.*, I, i, p. 571), an error repeated by Cooper, *Athenae*, i, p. 260. For
Wisdom's life during this period, see my article: "Robert Wisdom under
Persecution, 1541-1543" in the *Journal of Ecclesiastical History*, Vol. II, No. 2
(1951) pp. 180-189

c

Foxe is no less inaccurate in his reference to Becon. We know that Becon made his first recantation about this time, but before June, 1541, he had retired into Kent. His clash with the authorities, therefore, must have occurred in April or early May at the latest—two months, that is, before Bonner took action against Wisdom. In making Becon recant with Wisdom, Foxe appears to have been thinking of their submission together at Paul's Cross two years later. As to the rest of the statement, Becon may have been made to burn the heretical books in his possession—he had at this time written nothing of his own, however, which could be confiscated.

Let us turn now to Becon's evidence. In his second recantation he refers to his first :

> I . . . have in the countreyes of Norff. and Suff. three yeres paste wyllyngly and truylye knowledged in opyn sermons, that I hadd before that day preached and taughte evyll and false doctryne unto them, whiche my Recantation as I made yt ys conteyned at leingith in this booke.[1]

This admission, made in July, 1543, implies that he was first presented for heresy in the summer of 1540. His chronology, however, is rarely accurate, and " three yeres paste " probably means that at some time during 1540 he was called to account and made to submit. This would be roughly consistent with Foxe's statement that Becon recanted at the time of the persecution in February, 1540-41 ; he may even have been one of those who were brought before the commission—though not in company with Wisdom.

Becon, then, was apprehended on account of sermons which he had preached in the diocese of Norwich ; he was compelled to recant, and perhaps to burn his books, sometime during February or March, 1540-1 ; and was required to publish his submission in " opyn sermons " in the places where he had preached—which he did, he says, " wyllyngly and truylye." Then, before June, 1541, he managed quietly to disappear, and sought an asylum in Kent.

No copy of Becon's first recantation is extant, but we know something of its contents from the references which he makes to it in his second. This appears to contain, not a reproduction

---

[1] See Becon's second recantation, printed in full in Foxe, v, App. XII.

of the recantation " at leingith", but a recapitulation of its main points, as follows :

> I shall declare unto you some specyalties . . . of myne owne preachinge whiche a greate number of Norff. and Suff. knowe. . . . I have preached agaynste the praynge unto saincts untruylie. I have preached againste the contynencie of prysts untruylye. I have preached againste prayer for the deade untruylie. I have preached so of the Sacrament of Thaltare as men were offended with me. I have preached also to the derogation and derysion of the Sacraments of confirmation and extreme unction. And all thys same have I doon under the name of Thomas Becon prieste. Whereof I am ryghte sory ; and have heretofore under the same name of Thomas Becon made Recantation which ys here (as I have saide) in this booke worde for worde.

The original recantation may have been more explicit, but the admissions as they stand do not indicate precisely what was considered offensive in Becon's opinions. The charges are only general and typical of those commonly preferred against the " heretics " ; they occur repeatedly in Foxe's accounts of the persecutions at this time. Only two contravene the Six Articles Act : to preach against clerical celibacy was contrary to the third article, and the first was worded so comprehensively as to bring under censure all who " by any means condemn, deprave, or despise the said blessed Sacrament "[1] and thereby cause offence, as Becon seems to have done. There is nothing to distinguish him from the other humble offenders who were presented at about the same time, but being a preacher and in orders, he was made to recant.

[1] See Gee and Hardy, *Documents*, p. 307.

CHAPTER III

RETIREMENT INTO KENT, 1541-1543

I

W HEN Becon made his way into Kent, he probably did
so at the suggestion of friends, and may have carried
introductions to some of the gentry with protestant
sympathies to whom he later dedicated his first works. No
doubt he hoped to find peace and even covert encouragement
in the diocese of Thomas Cranmer, but, as he tells us in his
second recantation, he went cautiously and took no risks :

> . . . I chaunged my dwellinge, and leavinge that Country [Norfolk
> and Suffolk] repayred unto Kent where I have lurked ever syns.
> I chaunged myne Apparel and shewyd myne self lyke a layman.
> I chaunged also my name, and callid my self Theodore Basile.
> I chaunged the forme of teachinge the people frome preachinge
> unto wrytynge.

This retirement seems to have been something more than a
prudent withdrawal into the country to escape further attention.
Becon's methods of self-concealment are too deliberate and
elaborate for that. He had made his submission ; why was it
necessary to adopt a disguise and a feigned name, and to
" lurk " in parts where he was almost unknown ? And why,
having publicly renounced his former errors, should he proceed
forthwith to resume his heretical activities and teach the people
by writing ?

All this suggests that Becon may have been acting according
to a pre-arranged plan, and that the supporters of the
Reformation in East Anglia who had encouraged his preaching
were now trying to secure his continued usefulness to their
cause by obtaining for him an asylum from which he could
issue the tracts which were to be his new form of teaching. For
this purpose Kent was admirable. He would be in Cranmer's
diocese, within easy reach of the capital and his publisher,
among reliable favourers of the new learning, yet in parts

where he would pass unrecognized. His change of name and apparel would facilitate the working of the scheme, and are not easily explained on other grounds, as he would not have been in any real danger had he chosen to refrain from interference in religious affairs.

Accordingly, in June, 1541, or thereabout we find Becon being entertained by Sir Thomas Neville of Mereworth, whose hospitality and good-will were acknowledged by the dedication of a work composed for the following Christmas—*A Christmas Banquet*—in the preface to which he mentions sitting at the knight's table " before six months past ".[1] A second work soon appeared—*A Potation for Lent*—again inscribed to Sir Thomas, who had rewarded Becon's first tribute with " singular beneficence and grand liberality ".[2] These, however, were not his first compositions, for he had already written *The News out of Heaven*, which he inscribed to another patron, George Pierpount, as a new year's gift in recognition of the latter's " most bounteous gentleness ".[3]

The News out of Heaven is simply a cento of biblical passages relating to man's redemption through Christ, and shows to advantage Becon's favourite method of allowing scripture to speak for itself, piling text upon text and illustration upon illustration, and relying for effect upon the selection and arrangement of his material.

The *Christmas Banquet* is the first of seven dialogues between *Philemon* (who usually represents Becon himself), *Theophile*, *Eusebius*, and *Christopher*. The last three, neighbours of *Philemon*, are invited to a spiritual repast at which four texts are served as dishes.[4] The host instructs and exhorts his guests in Christian doctrine and duty, while they, from time to time, interject questions, observations, and expressions of approval. Then, having fed their souls with this " celestial banquet of God's word ", all retire to partake at *Philemon's* board of " such poor repast for the sustenance of [the] body, as it hath pleased God to prepare . . ."[5]

---

[1] P i, p. 61.
[2] P i, p. 88.
[3] P i, p. 44.
[4] Gen. iii. 17, 18 ; Gen. iii. 15 ; Mark i. 15 ; Eph. ii. 10.
[5] P i, p. 84.

The *Potation*, written during February or March, 1541-2, is an exposition of the sacrament of Penance ; it contains a section on fasting and an explanation of the church ceremonies customary in Lent, and concludes with instruction on preparation for the Communion. It is the most conservative of all Becon's works, and the one most extensively revised for the folio edition, and certain features in it will be discussed in the next chapter.

Two more compositions soon followed. The *Pathway unto Prayer* treats in fifty-three short chapters of the nature and methods of prayer, which, to the author, means chiefly petition and intercession. *A Pleasant New Nosegay*, written in May, 1542, is another work in dialogue form, consisting of dissertations upon five " flowers " : Unfeigned Humility, Pure Innocence, Faithful Obedience, Ready Assistance, and Christian Charity. In it the reader is taught his duty towards God, his neighbour, and " our most puissant and excellent king". This book is dedicated to George Whetnall who, with his son Thomas, joined the exiles in Frankfort in December, 1554, and at one stage took a minor part in the Prayer Book controversy there.[1] His connexion by marriage with other patrons of Becon is shown in Genealogical Table 2.

II

By August, 1542, it seemed that war with France was imminent, and Kent was the scene of extensive military preparations, some fifteen or twenty thousand men being assembled there to await embarkation. This martial activity around him moved Becon to consider what he could do in the emergency, and the result was the composition of a " little treatise", *The New Policy of War*, later renamed *The True Defence of Peace*, which he dedicated to the poet and soldier Sir Thomas Wyatt. In it he extols the virtue of patriotism, denounces such as Reginald Pole who were not ashamed to

[1] Garrett, *Exiles*, p. 324 ; *Troubles*, p. xxvi.

A newe

pathway vnto prai
er, ful of much godly frute
and christê knowledge,
lately made by Thé
odore Basille.

✱

Psal. 6.

Delyght thou in the Lord
and he shal gyue the, the
peticions of thy
herte.

write *Roma est mihi patria*, and praises the public spirit shown
by the gentlemen and commons of Kent.[1] His purpose is to
declare

> . . . in how pitiful a case the christian public weal consisteth
> almost universally . . .
>
> . . . what is the cause of these cruel wars that reign now almost
> throughout the whole world, and by what means they may be
> ceased . . .
>
> . . . after what manner we may get the victory of our enemies . . .
>
> . . . how the soldiers ought to behave themselves . . . [and also]
> they that tarry at home . . .
>
> . . . how christian men shall return from the wars after they have
> gotten the victory, and on what manner they shall behave them-
> selves, that their country may enjoy peace and tranquillity ever
> after.[2]

He deplores the lamentable dissention among Christian princes,
especially when it leads to so unholy an alliance as that between
the King of France and the " great Turk".[3] Nor does he spare
his own land, condemning not only its sin, but also the reactionary spirit which scorns the benefits of reformation and
hankers after a return to the old order which is passing. He
denounces the pillaging, gambling, swearing, and immorality
of the average soldier, and the lack of responsibility in those
who remain at home, especially when they corner the wheat
market until they can force up the prices.[4] He pleads, too, for
the appointment of chaplains to minister to the soldiery.[5]
Throughout his book, which must have been written between
the issue of the orders for enlistment on 10th August, and
Wyatt's death on 3rd October, 1542, the theme of Becon's
exhortation to his countrymen is that, while due preparation
in the face of the emergency must not be neglected, the nation's
destiny is always in the hands of God, and only those who serve
him faithfully can hope for victory and peace.

Several other works belong to this period. *David's Harp*, a
verse-by-verse exposition of Psalm 115,[6] appeared in 1542, but

---

[1] P i, pp. 233, 235.
[2] P i, pp. 235-236.
[3] P i, p. 239.
[4] P i, p. 253.
[5] P i, p. 252.
[6] i.e., Ps. cxvi. 10-19, Authorised Version.

its exact date of composition is unknown.[1] In his preface to the folio edition Becon mentions a metrical *Catechism* of which only some prefatory verses and a single line[2] have survived. In its place he wrote, in 1559 or 1560, another *Catechism* in prose "both long and large", to which he prefixed the verses just mentioned. Nothing is known of the metrical *Catechism*, though it appears among the books prohibited by the proclamation of 8th July, 1546.

Coverdale had translated Bullinger's *Der Christlich Eestand* (published in Zurich, in 1540) and this, Becon says, was

> . . . for the more ready sale, set forth in my name by the hungry printer with my preface, to make it the more plausible to the readers.[3]

It was first entitled *The Golden Book of Christian Matrimony*, and was later re-issued as *The Christian State of Matrimony*. In his second recantation Becon seems to assume responsibility for the whole book, and not simply the preface, for he says, ". . . in all that booke I exhorte all men to marrage indifferentelye . . ." When preparing the folio edition, he wrote a treatise of his own on the subject, retaining, with a new concluding paragraph, the preface which stands in the editions of Coverdale's translation.

Another work, listed in the proclamation of 8th July, 1546, of which nothing is known is a collection of *Christmas Carols* published under the name of Theodore Basille,[4] and undoubtedly written in Kent. In December, 1542, Becon composed a third dialogue, *A New Year's Gift*, declaring

> . . . what a precious treasure Christ is unto us, which was given us of God the Father for our new-year's gift, and how many benefits we have received by him.[5]

An Invective against Swearing concludes the works known to have been written by him during his sojourn in Kent.

---

[1] Ritson, who obviously had not seen it, says that it " is presumed to have been in metre " : *Bib. Poet.*, p. 128.

[2] " Gravyn ymages shall then non make", quoted in Becon's second recantation.

[3] P i, p. 29 ; see also Bullinger's *Decades* (PS), v, p. xviii.

[4] See Foxe, v, p. 567, n. 2.

[5] P i, p. 307.

III

All these compositions were printed for the publisher, John Gough, by John Mayler, a member of the Grocers' Company, " a scholar, and a zealous man for the Reformation", who had himself been presented at the time of the second persecution under the Six Articles in 1540-41 as " a sacramentary, and a railer against the mass".[1] In all, eleven treatises or poems (some of the former, of considerable length) and a long preface, as well as prayers and slighter works, issued from Becon's industrious pen in less than two years, and his popularity as a writer is evident from the fact that during this period twenty editions of his own books and two of Coverdale's *Matrimony* (which he had virtually sponsored) were published. *A Christmas Banquet* even appeared in a German translation.[2] No wonder Mayler found that " Basille's " name on the title-page made a book " the more plausible to the readers ", and secured " a more ready sale".

From the descriptions which have been given it will be seen that these works are mainly hortatory and devotional, and emphasize the practical aspects of Christian belief and duty. They are not designedly controversial, though running through most of them is a note of protestant apologetic. Becon expresses great satisfaction at the progress of the Reformation and the state of religion in the country, due mainly to the " divine policy and godly enterprise " of Henry, " our most virtuous and godly king".[3] Now, he says,

> All false religion is extirpated and plucked up by the roots. The miserable captivity, wherewith we were oppressed in the pope's kingdom, is turned into delectable liberty. Our consciences are restored to their old freedom. . . .[4]

To object against such a eulogy that in fact one tyranny had only been exchanged for another, and that the writer seems to have forgotten that he was in hiding because of the denial of the very liberty of conscience which he praises, is to overlook the protestant habit of attributing measures of oppression or

---

[1] Foxe, v, p. 445 ; he is reported to have said that " the mass was called, beyond the sea, *miss*, for that all is *amiss* in it " : Ames, *Typ. Ant.*, iii, p. 541.
[2] Bib. I, A 3b.
[3] Preface to the *Nosegay*, P i, p. 193.
[4] *A New Pathway unto Prayer*, ch. xlvii, P i, p. 181.

persecution to the malign influence of " papists " and of clerical conservatives like Gardiner and Bonner.[1] The king himself, Becon was sure, stood on the side of those who supported the Reformation, and was about to inaugurate a golden age in England.[2] It was not long, however, before this sanguine hope was dashed by the catholic reaction with which the reign of the Supreme Head closed.

Despite religious reforms, Becon complains that offences of every kind against God and man continue to abound in England. The Commandments are repeatedly transgressed, and there are many signs of indifference abroad. Instead of gathering together on Sunday and holyday afternoons to make merry, as was the custom, he would have the " common sort of people " occupied " in fervent prayers, or else in the reading or hearing of the holy scriptures".[3] As it is, they run to the taverns and alehouses immediately the service is ended—if, indeed, they were not to be found there before it began. Negligent clergy are common,[4] although even when the people have

. . . a ghostly and learned curate, which according to his office would be glad to teach them the will of God, him do they hate, they wish the pulpit a coal-pit. They think it a hundred year, if he preacheth but half an hour. . . .[5]

A similar spirit exists among the gentry, with their " gallant pomp and lascivious pleasures",[6] and their craze for fine clothes.

The tailors now-a-days are compelled to excogitate, invent, and imagine diversities of fashions for apparel, that they may satisfy the foolish desire of certain light brains and wild oats, which are altogether given to newfangledness. . . . Sometime we follow the fashion of the Frenchmen. Another time we will have a trick of the Spaniards. Shortly after that beginneth to wax naught : we must therefore now have the Italian fashion. Within a few days after we are weary of all the fashions that are used in christendom ; we will therefore now, and God will, practise the manner of going among the Turks and Saracens. . . .[7]

[1] See on this, Dixon, HCE, ii, p. 404 and n.†
[2] *A New Pathway unto Prayer*, ch. xlviii ; P i, p. 182.
[3] *An Invective against Swearing*, P i, p. 362.
[4] *The New Policy of War*, P i, pp. 254-255 ; cf *An Invective against Swearing*, preface, P i, pp. 353-354.
[5] Prologue to *News out of Heaven*, P i, p. 39.
[6] *The New Policy of War*, P i, p. 263.
[7] *A Pleasant New Nosegay*, P i, p. 204.

While the frivolous adorned their persons, the devout protestants preferred to decorate their houses in a godly style. " Here," exclaims *Christopher*, in *A Christmas Banquet*, as he enters *Philemon's* hall, " here nothing is dumb, all things speak " ; scriptural texts are placed everywhere. Upon the parlour door appear the words,

I am the door. By me if any man entereth in, he shall be safe, and shall go in and out, and shall find pasture ;

upon the chimney,

The fire of them shall not be quenched ;

in the window,

I am the light of the world . . . ;

upon the table,

Blessed is he that eateth bread in the kingdom of heaven.

Cups and dishes, chairs and stools, laver and virginals—all bear appropriate inscriptions.[1] So impressed were *Philemon's* guests that they proceeded to adorn their dwellings in like manner,[2] and Becon had no doubt seen the houses of some of his friends similarly garnished.[3]

There were some who found it advantageous to display a measure of sympathy with the Reformation, and during the ascendancy of Cromwell, with the dissolution of the monasteries in full flood, their show of enthusiasm proved not unprofitable. But the lives of these " gross gospellers", as Becon calls them, belied their professions, and he urges them to mend their ways.[4]

Nothing moves Becon to more fervent expressions of thankfulness than the fact that the Bible could now be freely read in English. But this " incomparable benefit " was not appreciated. The royal injunctions of 1538 had ordered " one book of the whole Bible of the largest volume, in English " to be set up " in some convenient place " within each parish church, yet Becon asks,

[1] *A Christmas Banquet*, P i, pp. 63-66.

[2] *A Potation* . . ., P i, pp. 89-90.

[3] For other examples of this, see A. L. Maycock, *Nicholas Ferrar*, p. 149 ; F. D. How, *The Life of Archbishop Maclagan*, pp. 28 and 200; A. C. Benson, *The Life of Edward White Benson*, i, p. 577.

[4] See *The New Policy of War*, P i, pp. 256-257 ; *A Potation* . . . (of Fasting), P i, p. 104 ; *David's Harp* (ninth string), P i, p. 293.

. . . how many read it ? Verily, a man may come into some churches, and see the bible so inclosed and wrapped about with dust, even as the pulpit in like manner is both with dust and cobwebs, that with his finger he may write upon the bible, this epitaph : *Ecce, nunc in pulvere dormio.* . . .[1]

Christ's scholar, he says in *A New Year's Gift*, must love and study the Word of God, and exhort others to do the same,[2] but a marginal note at this point in the first edition, afterwards omitted, states that

. . . in Paul's church may a man see the leaves of the bible torn out, and that no small number ; and all because men should have no knowledge of God's word : neither do men love the readers thereof, but seek with all guile to persecute them and cast them in prison ; so that in a short time they die . . .

This note is unfair, however, in its implications. The truth is that the privilege of the open vernacular Bible had been abused otherwise than by neglect. Not content with reading it quietly, some took it upon themselves to read aloud, to gather an audience and expound—and this, even during divine service. Several of the presentations under the Six Articles at the end of 1540 were for this offence, contrary to the royal injunctions[3] and Bonner's very reasonable admonitions.[4] Becon's note probably refers to John Porter, who about this time was committed to prison, where he died, for disobeying these orders —" cruelly martyred," says Foxe, " for reading the Bible in Paul's."[5]

Described by Wentworth as " a great setter forth . . . of the king's . . . supremacy", Becon is sometimes fulsome in his adulation of Henry VIII, " a prince of most noble fame and immortal glory",[6] and professes himself very sensible of the benefits enjoyed by those fortunate enough to live under the beneficent rule of the Supreme Head.[7] Like the rest of the reformers, he drew his views of the nature and function of the

---

[1] Prologue, *News out of Heaven*, P i, p. 38.
[2] P i, p. 322.
[3] See Burnet, *Reformation*, iv, pp. 507-508.
[4] ibid, p. 509 ; Foxe, v, App. XIV.
[5] Foxe, v, pp. 451-452.
[6] *A Christmas Banquet*, P i, p. 82.
[7] *A Pleasant New Nosegay*, preface, P i, p. 193.

secular power from the polity of the Hebrews as exemplified
in the Old Testament :

> To show that the authority of the magistrates and common
> officers is the ordinance of God, whereof may I rather take a
> beginning than of the public weal of the Israelites ?[1]

Accordingly, he expounds a high doctrine of the divinely
appointed status of kings and magistrates, illustrated by
examples of the " godly prince " from David to Josiah. Following a convention of the day in his exegesis of Psalm lxxxii. 6 :
" I said, ye are gods . . .", he asks,

> Doth not God here plainly say, that the magistrates are gods,
> that is, such as bear the offices of God. . . .?[2]

and a little later,

> . . . their judging place is the throne of God. Their mouth and
> sentence is the organ and instrument of God's truth. They are
> the vicars of God. They are the livish image of God. They are
> the ministers of God for our wealth. They represent the person
> of God. They exercise the judgment of the Lord. . . .[3]

In particular, Becon will allow no ecclesiastical privilege :

> . . . there is not one bishop or priest within this realm of England,
> which oweth not so much obedience to the king's grace's majesty,
> as the most inferior subject and vile temporal man doth. . . .
> There is none excepted, no, not that Romish pork, which chal-
> lengeth so great authority over all persons in the world. . . .[4]

In the past there had undoubtedly been " great abusion in the
clergy concerning temporal rulers", but he thanks God for the
revelation of the truth concerning authority, which has enabled
certain princes to assert their rights.[5] At the same time he
laments that even in England the king's lawful supremacy is
not universally recognized. It is denied by the Anabaptists
(against whom it was safe for anyone to turn his hand or his
pen),[6] and there are " seditious persons " abroad, who are

[1] *A Pleasant New Nosegay*, preface, P i, p. 211.

[2] ibid, P i, p. 212.

[3] ibid, P i, p.215 ; *cf David's Harp* (fourth string), P i, p. 277 ; *An Invective against Swearing*, P i, p. 370 ; *A New Catechism*, P ii, pp. 307 and 327. See also Bradford, *Meditation on the Passion, Works* (PS), ii, pp. 254-255 ; Sandys, *Sermon* xii, *Works* (PS), p. 225 ; Tyndale, *The Obedience of a Christian Man, Works* (PS), i, p. 175 ; Whitgift, *Works* (PS), ii, pp. 82-83.

[4] ibid, P i, p. 216.

[5] ibid, P i, p. 217.

[6] ibid ; the Anabaptists had no theory of clerical privilege, but simply denied that the state had any rights in the sphere of conscience.

" without any godly fear toward the public magistrates". To the latter Becon utters a warning :

> . . . what, I pray you, hath ever been muttered or secretly conspired against the king's grace's majesty at any time, either among men of nobility, or yet of the baser sort, that hath not come to light, and wrought destruction to the authors thereof ? This is undoubtedly the provision of God. . . . For as it is impossible to hinder or let the course of the sun or moon, so it is impossible for them to escape which imagine or work any violence or treason against his grace.[1]

With a Privy Council in constant session and its agents active throughout the land in detecting and tracing to its source anything that could be brought within a wide definition of treason, men were only too well aware of these things. So *Philemon*, with no less prudence than patriotism, explains to his friends their duty to the king and his magistrates.

IV

We do not know where Becon dwelt during these two years in Kent, but he probably found shelter in the house of one of the gentry sympathetic to the Reformation. Straitened in circumstances, as usual, he describes his possessions at this time as " not worth a gally half-penny besides a few books and a little slender apparel".[2] He resumed his teaching duties, probably as a private tutor, and says that the *Nosegay* was

> . . . gathered of me in the space of a few days, at such hours as I could conveniently suffurate and steal away from the institution and teaching of my scholars.[3]

Not only did he change his clothes, but he seems to have relinquished all exercise of his priestly duties. He does not refer to his orders, and in the preface-dedicatory to *The New Policy of War* he poses as a man of letters " trained up from my cradles in the court of Lady Mnemosyne and her daughters, and exercised in the wrestling-place of Apollo",[4] possibly with the object of commending himself and his work to Wyatt.

---

[1] *A Pleasant New Nosegay*, preface, P i, p. 218.
[2] *The New Policy of War*, preface, P i, p. 235 and n. 6.
[3] *A Pleasant New Nosegay*, preface, P i, p. 195.
[4] P i, p. 236.

Soon after completing the *Nosegay* Becon was afflicted with " grievous and troublous sicknesses ", though of what kind he does not say.[1] He also implies that at the same time he had other difficulties with which to contend, and which caused him no little vexation. Writing, probably in December, 1542, the first pages of *A New Year's Gift*, he says :

> . . . I . . . have been so turmoiled and vexed with the cares and troubles of this world for the space of six or seven months, that I have had no leisure almost once to think of the holy scripture . . .[2]

We know nothing of the " divers businesses " which had so disquieted him that he confesses to a certain " dissolution and slackness ", but they may not have been unconnected with the events which brought his retirement in Kent to an end.

[1] *A New Year's Gift*, preface, P i, p. 308.
[2] ibid, P i, p. 309.

CHAPTER IV

SECOND RECANTATION, 1543

I

THE publication in May, 1543, of the King's Book, or *A Necessary Doctrine and Erudition for any Christian Man*, marked a decided stiffening of Henry's anti-protestant policy, and a third persecution under the Six Articles followed. On 28th July three heretics were burned in front of Windsor Castle, while John Merbeck, fortunately for the music of the English Church, received a royal pardon. Before the Windsor martyrs had passed to the stake, a timely recantation saved Becon from their fate, and with him at Paul's Cross on Relics Sunday, 8th July, his old friend Wisdom and one Robert Singleton also abjured.[1]

Proceedings had begun against Wisdom more than two months before, but we do not know when action was first taken against Becon. It is doubtful whether his pseudonym deceived the authorities for long, and his activities had probably been under observation for some time.[2] Wisdom seems inadvertently to have attracted attention to him in a sermon, for in his recantation Becon says :

> And here I mighte saye somewhat to maister Wysedome here
> presente howe moche was he deceaved or howe moche wente he

---

[1] See Wriothesley's *Chronicle*, i, pp. 142-143. The date assigned to these recantations in L & P. Henry VIII, xviii, pt. i, No. 538, pp. 313-314 (14th May) is wrong. On that date Wisdom had recognizances taken, see Foxe, v, App. XII, and he would not have been made to recant as well. He himself is not more accurate, for in his revocation he gives the date of his recantation as " the xiiij day of July ", in 1543, a Saturday, and not Relic Sunday, as he says ; see Foxe, v, App. XXII*.

[2] In this connexion it is interesting to note that Becon's printer, Mayler, was one of eight members of that trade who were committed to prison on 8th April, 1543, "for printing off suche bokes as wer thowght to be unlawfull, contrary to the proclamation made on that behalf". On 22nd April, with four others, he was released, on condition that they made a declaration of the books they had bought and sold during the previous three years, and four days later they lodged certificates accordingly; see J. R. Dasent (ed.), *Acts of the Privy Council*, 1542-1547, pp. 107 and 117.

aboute to deceave the good people, to call me opynly in his
sermon made at Aldermarye in Lent last paste The man of godd,
who have continuallye laboured in the service of the Dyvell,
preaching untruylye by the name of Thomas Becon, and wrytyng
untruylye by the name of Theodore basile. I mervaile maister
Wysedom abhorred nott this Spyryte of pryde to make my
wrytings equall with the sacred bible and goddis worde.[1]

He must have submitted to examination, but no records of
this are extant.

Wisdom began the recantations with the reading of a
" shameful bill that Winchester devised", and handed out
signed copies of his statement. Then came Becon's turn.
First, as we have seen, he told how he had preached heresy in
Norfolk and Suffolk, how he had recanted, and how he had
disguised himself and had hidden in Kent. Next, he confessed
his pride :

I fynde yt worshipfull Audyence in the experyence of my self
moost true, that as saincte Jamys saith Deus superbis resistit
God resisteth the proude. I have been possessed with the spyryte
of pryde and vayne glorye, and nourysshed therewith have
indured theese labours, to wryte suche bookes as have goon
fourthe under the name of Theodore Basile. First my newe
counterfaite name, Theodore basile whiche ys as moche to say,
as a kynge gyven of Godd, ys yt not a proude name to be of myne
owne chosynge . . .

Again,

. . . ye shall fynde in dyverse parties of my bookes greeke woordes
made Englyshe as Encomion for a praise mnemosinon for a
Remembraunce and suche other monstrouse woordes for the
Reader to wonder at, and wrytten onely by me, for vayne glorye
to doo the Reader understande that I were learned in the greeke
tonge, wherein I confesse playnely I am not learned at all.

As the crowning example of this spirit, he cited a paragraph
from the prologue to *News out of Heaven* :

I will not praise the book, lest I should seem to hunt after vain
glory ; neither will I dispraise it, lest I might seem rashly and
without a cause to condemn that which is worthy praise and
commendation of itself. . . . This I dare boast, that it containeth
more true and christian learning than a great sort of volumes
that we have highly esteemed in times past. He that shall make
this book his companion shall here find in few leaves that the whole

---

[1] Foxe, v, App. XII, where the recantation is printed in full, with those
of Wisdom and Singleton.

D

bible and commentaries of the ancient doctors do teach of Christ
in many, so that it might well be called *the treasurehouse of
christian knowledge*.   Neither can any man justly condemn or
reject this book, except he also will condemn and set at nought
the most sacred and holy bible . . .[1]

Becon then went on to make certain specific retractions. First,
he recapitulated the substance of his earlier recantation.[2]
Then he took copies of eleven of his books, cited from each a
passage to which objection had been taken, and then cut the
offending volume in pieces. Finally he renounced his doctrine
in general :

And besyde theese specialties whiche I cannot with any excuse
avoyde, the good woordes in my bookes, suche as well placed and
ordered mighte be spoken, bee of my singularitie and vanytie
soo set forthe as they mighte gyve occasion (yf credyte were
hadde to the Autor) to maintayne many suche naughtie and
pestyferous opynyons as hathe been of late sooed amongs the
people.   And therefore I wyshe here all my bookes destroyed
accordynge to the kynges maiestyes proclamations as theese be
here destroyed with myne owne handes.   And to thentent noo
man shulde mysraporte what I have saied I have signed dyverse
copyes of that I nowe reherse with myne owne hands.   Whereof
eche man may have the copye that will.

So ended Becon's recantation, and the proceedings terminated
with a brief abjuration by Singleton.

II

Becon's " specialties " are eighteen in number, collected
out of nine different works. They are presumably passages to
which the authorities had taken exception, and upon which he
may have been examined. Four imply criticism of the measures
taken to enforce doctrinal uniformity, and would hardly be
regarded as calculated to promote quietness and unanimity in
matters of religion :

. . . as they persecuted the prophetes and true preachers of goddis
woorde,[3] evyn soo doo they nowe :[4] in which I seme tapprove

[1] P i, p. 43.
[2] See above, p 17.
[3] " verity " in folio ed.
[4] *The New Policy of War*, see P i, p. 242

the cause of suche as have been justelye punyshed by the ordre
of the kinges maiestye lawes. Which be onely suche as have
preached or taughte false doctryne . . .
. . . I bydde men marke that Thapostles saiede wee cannot doo
none otherwyse but speake . . .[1]
. . . as good woorks folowe fayeth so dothe persecution folowe the
confession of goddis woorde. . . . Chrystes woorde and the crosse
be companyons inseparable, and as the shadowe folowith the
bodye soo dothe the crosse folowe the woorde of chryste and as
fyer and heate cannot be separated, soo cannot the woorde of
chryste and the crosse be plucked asonder. In whiche woordes
I doo not onely noughtelie affirm the necessytie of goode workynge
of suche as be in faythe,[2] but also falselye and sedytyously saye
that evyn amongste goode chrysten men the doctryne whiche ys
not contynually persecuted with the crosse (as I call yt) cannot
be the true doctryne of chryste.[3]
. . . speakinge of the confession of oure faythe I say mooste
sedytiouslie theese woordes folowinge, noo menacyng woordes
noo imprisonmente noo cheynes noo fetters no swerd no faggot
no fyer oughte to plucke us from this confession no tyrannie
oughte soo to be feared that godd and his truyth shulde not be
confessed :[4] as thoughe theese punyshments were used againste
the true confession of faythe.

Other passages on grace, faith, and good works have a
distinctly Lutheran flavour. Becon makes faith the " foundation and ground of the christian religion",[5] and asserts that
" Faith in Christ alone saveth".[6] This leads him to maintain,
as did many Lutherans, that good works necessarily and
inevitably spring from faith, so that the latter becomes the
principle, not simply of justification, but of the whole Christian
life. For instance :

In my booke of a Chrystmasse bankett I say the gyftes of grace
cannot be ydle.[7] Whiche ys contrarye to Sainte Paule, desyrynge
the Corynthyans that they will not receave the grace of godd in
vayne. And in the same booke I say also that yt ys impossible

[1] *David's Harp* (second string), see P i, p. 271 ; the reference is to Acts iv,
and especially verse 20.
[2] For further examples of this, see below.
[3] *David's Harp* (third string), see P i, p. 273.
[4] *A Potation* . . . (of Confession), see P i, p. 99.
[5] *A Pleasant New Nosegay* (second flower), P i, p. 207.
[6] *A Christmas Banquet* (third dish), marg. n., P i, p. 79 ; *cf A New
Pathway unto Prayer*, xvi, P i, p. 147, and *David's Harp* (first string), P i,
pp. 269-270.
[7] See P i, p. 80—in the folio ed., " . . . the gifts of virtues cannot be idle",
a quotation from a work attributed to Ambrose, see n. 2.

for true faythe to be without goode woorkes,[1] a faythfull man, whiche is the sonne of Godd.[2] Thys ys daungerouslye and falselye spooken to mantayne the abhominable opynyon of necessitie, whiche is neyther in vice ne vertue.

. . . a Christen man settyng before his eyes the unmeasurable goodnes of godd and gyvyng earneste faythe thereto cannot otherwyse but love god agayne and take all meanes possible to please hym, to woork hys wyll, and to doo that whiche he requyreth of hym.[3]

. . . as he that hathe the true and perfecte sighte of the eyes stumbleth nott but walketh at all tymes without daunger. soo in lyke maner he that ys endued by christs spyrytt with the lighte of holye scryptures wandereth not from chryste, And that Satan with all his Armye are not able once to abduce and remove hym from the true wayes for the lighte of godds woorde ys contynually before his eyes.[4] In whiche woordes I torne the promisse made by oure Savyoure Chryste to his churche unto every faythfull man as thoughe he whiche were ones faithful coulde noo more be over come with the devill and comytte deadly synne : falselye.

These passages plainly contradict the teaching of the *Necessary Doctrine and Erudition for any Christian Man*,[5] as also[6] does his denunciation of images :

In my booke of a newe Cathecism I saye that godd commaundeth we shall make noo gravyn ymage. Theese be my woordes, Gravyn ymages shall then non make. Which my woordes soo spoken against ymages as thoughe all ymages were unlawfull I myself doo condempne.[7]

Two extracts from Becon's works censure the following of men's traditions rather than the scriptures :

I forbydde . . . the teachinge of all mennys tradycions (as I call them), and will men having spirituall chardge to teache onelye the scryptures and suche thinges, whereof the holy gooste ys the Authoure, contempnyng arrogantelye all other teachings . . .[8]

---

[1] This may not be a quotation ; I have failed to trace the actual words, but the idea occurs frequently in the *Banquet, cf* this, from the " fourth dish " : ". . . good works necessarily follow the christian faith . . . as the shadow followeth the body, and death the life", P i, p. 79.

[2] This again cannot be found, but Becon says in the *Banquet* (third dish) : " By faith are we made the sons of God", P i, p. 79.

[3] *David's Harp* (second string), P i, p. 271.

[4] *A Pleasant New Nosegay*, preface, see P i, p. 192.

[5] *Formularies*, p. 367.

[6] ibid, p. 299.

[7] It may be observed that in the conservative *Potation* Becon writes of the veiling of the images during Lent, and says nothing there directly in condemnation of them.

[8] *An Invective against Swearing*, see P i, p. 382.

In my booke callid the potation I say theese woordes They that teache any other thinges than the scryptures teache not chrysten but humayne inventions.[1]

Two others, contrary to the Six Articles[2] and the King's Book,[3] " exhorte all men to marrage indifferentelye ; makynge noo difference whether they bee pryests or noo " :

Let other prayse suche as maye justelye seame to be monstrouse of nature for theire steryllitie and barrennes ; yet will I commende them, whiche according to theire fyrst creation and the naturall dysposition, that godd from the begynnynge engraffed in them are fructefull as a plentuouse vyne.[4]

Let other prayse them whiche when they dye leave noo lyvynge and quycke testymonies behynde them ; yet will I commende them which when they gyve over to nature leave quyck and lyvynge testymonies behynde them wherebye they declare that they have lyved and not been [un]fructefull nor unprofitable to the christen publique weale.[5]

Yet two more passages simply reflect that " Spyryte of pryde " of which Becon had already made lengthy acknowledgment :

My faithe ys that I am wrytten in the booke of lyef.[6]

And in the same booke with lyke presumption as thoughe I were he of whom wolde ask accompte of all that perysshed in theire Tyme I say theese woordes folowyng, yf any man will not amende after this oure admonytion his dampnation fall upon his owne headd for I am free from his bloudde and have doon my duytie in that behalf.[7]

In *News out of Heaven*, after quoting certain prophetical denunciations of formal sacrifice unaccompanied by a change of heart, Becon says :

Here you see that God hath no pleasure in these external sacrifices, but rather abhorreth them.[8]

In the recantation his words appear with a slight but important alteration :

[1] See P i, p. 87.

[2] See Gee and Hardy, *Documents*, LXV, especially pp. 306, 310, and 318-319.

[3] *Formularies*, p. 293.

[4] See *The Christen State of Matrimony*, preface, fol. A ii verso—A iii recto = *The Book of Matrimony*, F i, fol. cccclxii recto.

[5] See *The Christen State of Matrimony*, fol. A iii verso=*The Book of Matrimony*, F i, fol. cccclxii verso.

[6] *An Invective against Swearing*, see P i, p. 356.

[7] ibid, see P i, p. 357.

[8] P i, p. 49.

> . . . godd hathe no pleasure in externall sacryfices but abhorreth them . . .

Thus he is made to condemn all outward or ritual sacrifices, and to imply that only inward, spiritual ones are acceptable to God. It might seem that here a retraction has been unfairly extorted, but reading further, we observe that Becon ignores those sacrifices which are the genuine expression of a truly penitent spirit. The authorities were quick to see that this omission could be turned to account. It gave them an opportunity to extract a statement upon the Mass, concerning which no heterodox opinions seem to have been detected in his writings, though it will be remembered that he had preached offensively about it. So he declares, as he had doubtless been directed :

> . . . albeit godd abhorreth ypocrysie, and ys not pleased with owtewarde Sacrifices where inwarde devotion wantieth, yet was godd highlye pleased with Abelles Sacryfice and ys nowe undoubtedlye moste hyghlye pleased with owre owtewarde celebration of the mooste high, pure, and excellent Sacryfice of the mooste bleassed Sacrament of Thaltare, wherein chryste hymself offereth hymself by the mynyster for a continuall memorye Reall and effectual of his oblation made at his laste supper and uppon the Crosse.

Some of the foregoing " specialties " are heretical, either definitely or in their tendency, and some reflect advanced views of Lutheran provenance. Others, however, and especially those which exhibit Becon's pride and vainglory, seem to have been selected simply with the object of discrediting him, and so weakening the influence which he wielded through writings which passed so rapidly into second and even third editions. And when no express retraction could be extorted, a declaration like the last, affirming a catholic view of the Mass, would itself be damaging to the protestant cause when made by so popular a writer.

There remain, however, two passages in the recantation which do not appear to deviate essentially from the standard of orthodoxy represented by the King's Book. In the *Potation*, Becon says :

> . . . I call satisfaction amendment of lyef whiche I never redde in scrypture nor auncyent doctours to be thexposition of satisfaction.[1]

[1] P i, p. 102.

Yet in *A Necessary Doctrine and Erudition for any Christian Man* both he and his accusers must have read that for the obtaining of the sacrament of penance " contrition, confession, and satisfaction " are needed,[1] and that the last, on man's side, consists principally in amendment of life.[2] Furthermore, Becon makes his meaning clear in words which distinctly resemble those of the formulary. Stating first that

> . . . Christ alone is the omnisufficient satisfaction for all our sins unto God the Father . . . there is no satisfaction perfect and sufficient . . . but only the death of Christ. . .

he goes on to insist that for Christ's work to avail for the penitent the latter must make his response :

> Whosoever repenteth him of his sins from the very heart, and is sorry for them, lamenteth his misery, hungereth for strength to do the will of God, knowledgeth his offences, laboureth with all main to walk in a new life . . . needeth not to doubt but that Christ by his death hath abundantly satisfied to God the Father for his sins.[3]

But satisfaction means more than this :

> . . . ye must then amend your life. . . . Ye must practice in your living all godliness and innocency. Fasting, prayer, and alms, must diligently be exercised of you. . . . These things done, then remaineth there a true and perfect satisfaction to our neighbour, whom we have offended or hurt either in word or deed.[4]

When it is remembered that shortly before these passages Becon had written (though somewhat guardedly) in favour of auricular confession, it is difficult to understand why exception should have been taken to a view of satisfaction so closely accordant with the teaching of the King's Book.

The second passage is also from the *Potation* :

> . . . Repetinge the thirde dysshe of my bankett [in the *Potation*[5]] I make two meanes onely tobtayne kyndnes at goddys hande repentaunce and beleaff, leaving owte the will to be confessid and to make satisfaction.

It is true that in the *Banquet* Becon says nothing of confession and satisfaction, but in the *Potation* there are separate sections on each, to which, in spite of his expository style and method,

[1] *Formularies*, p. 257.
[2] ibid, p. 260.
[3] *A Potation* . . ., P i, p. 102.
[4] ibid, P i, p. 103.
[5] See P i, p. 90.

objection could hardly be taken on the ground of heterodoxy. His offence here seems merely technical, and hardly justifies a retraction.

III

Becon's second recantation, however, leaves no doubt as to the Lutheran provenance of his ideas, and an examination of his " first period " writings affords further evidence of his protestant convictions.

We find, for instance, a strong emphasis upon man's desperately sinful plight and his utter incapacity for pleasing God, and upon the corresponding omnisufficiency of Christ as Saviour. Man is " utterly fallen from the favour of God " and " altogether without the Spirit of God"[1] :

> . . . not we only, but also all that ever we do of ourselves, is unpure and unclean in the sight of God, until both we and all our deeds be purified by the divine Spirit . . . [our deliverance from the bondage of sin] once done, then whatsoever we do in Christ and in our regeneration must needs be allowed before God, and received as an accepted sacrifice.[2]

Christ therefore is " the beginning and ending of all our salvation",[3] and both the " justiciaries "[4] and those who rely upon the merit earned by works of supererogation[5] stand condemned.[6] Only by faith can we experience and appropriate Christ's saving work accomplished once for all on our behalf ;[7] without it, " God's goodness profiteth us nothing at all".[8]

Again, Becon insists that scripture alone, " without any man's doctrine",[9] is sufficient for salvation, and is the only place where Christ and his truth can be learned.[10] The

---

[1] *News out of Heaven*, P i, p. 46.
[2] *David's Harp* (ninth string), P i, p. 292.
[3] *A Christmas Banquet* (second dish), P i, p. 75, marginal note.
[4] i.e., Pelagians, those who trust in their own capacity to attain righteousness ; see *News out of Heaven*, P i, p. 42 ; *A Potation* . . ., P i, p. 118 ; *A New Pathway unto Prayer*, vii, P i, p. 137.
[5] cf *A Christmas Banquet* (fourth dish), P i, p. 81 ; *A New Pathway unto Prayer*, lii, P i, p. 185.
[6] *A New Year's Gift*, P i, p. 312 ; see the whole passage: " Whosoever seeketh salvation . . . mystery of Christ's incarnation".
[7] *A Christmas Banquet* (third dish), P i, p. 79.
[8] *A New Pathway unto Prayer*, xvi, marg. n., P i, p. 147.
[9] ibid, v, P i, p. 134, marg. n.
[10] *A Potation* . . ., preface, P i, p. 87.

authorities would not overlook the fact that his works, with
their extensive biblical citations and incidental commentary
and exposition, were enabling the common people to continue
their reading of the Word of God as it were at second-hand,
just when the privilege of possessing and studying their own
Bibles had been denied them.

In his writings during 1541-1543 Becon so carefully avoided
the subject of the Mass that nothing objectionable on this
score was discovered in them, and the comparative leniency
with which he was treated was no doubt due to the fact that
he could not be branded a " sacramentary". For this omission
there was, as we shall see,[1] a good reason, but in any case, to
ignore the Mass entirely might be almost as effective as to
denounce it. Hence it is not mentioned in *A New Pathway unto
Prayer*, and the forms of public worship recommended in
The New Policy of War do not include any offering of the Mass.
During the time of fighting, sermons are prescribed, after which
the congregation are to " fall earnestly unto prayer " and
afterwards return quietly home. Similarly, when victory has
been won, " let the people gather together, and the preacher
make a solemn sermon unto them " ; this done, " let all the
people . . . with joyful voices sing hearty praises to our Lord
God".[2] The short section of the *Potation* which treats of the
Easter Mass at which the faithful communicated simply
emphasizes the need for due preparation and for thanksgiving
afterwards, and provides appropriate prayers.[3] Becon's inten-
tion in thus passing over the Mass would hardly be miscon-
strued, either by his sympathetic readers or by those on the
look-out for " heresy".

On the other hand there are features in these works to which
no exception could have been taken. We have already noticed
Becon's flattering eulogies of the king, his injunctions to
obedience, and his high doctrine of the civil power, and there
is almost a note of anxiety in his words at the end of the
Potation :

Above all things, as I have ever exhorted you, be obedient to
the king's grace's majesty, yea, and that not only for fear, but

[1] See below, p. 44.
[2] P i, p. 259.
[3] P i, pp. 117-121.

much more for conscience sake, in all things, as it becometh faithful subjects.

to which a marginal note adds emphasis :

Mark well for true obedience toward the king's gracious [1542 ed., grace's] majesty.[1]

In the *New Policy of War* he is at pains to declare his patriotism, and in the last chapter of the *New Pathway unto Prayer* he bids the pious reader pray

. . . for the preservation of the king's most excellent majesty, and for the prosperous success of his entirely beloved son, Edward our prince, that most angelic imp.[2]

And, contrasting the " true and christian fast " with the " popish and false fast " (which he represents as an indulgence in dainty living), he invokes the support of the royal theologian :

And because ye shall not doubt of this doctrine concerning fasting, know you, that the king's most royal majesty also, in his proclamation concerning eating of white meats this time of Lent, hath there no less prudently than godly set forth the very same thing, that hitherto I have taught you.[3]

Becon's views on auricular confession are also orthodox :[4]

Why auricular confession should be condemned and exiled from the bounds of christianity, I see no cause ; but that it should be approved, retained, and used, I find causes many, yea, and those right urgent and necessary.

It had certainly been abused in the past, but ought to be " restored to the old purity, and to the use for which it was first instituted."[5] He enlarges upon its advantages, explains the meaning of absolution (" a preaching of the free deliverance from all our sins through Christ's blood "[6]), and urges men to make their confessions in compliance with the orders of the Supreme Head.[7] The passages relating to auricular confession were retained when Becon revised the *Potation* for the folio

[1] P i, p. 121.
[2] Ch. lv, P i, p. 187.
[3] *A Potation* . . . (of fasting), P i, pp. 106-107. The Proclamation was issued on 6th February, 1541-2 (L & P Henry VIII, xvii, No. 85, p. 38) and repeated on 9th February, 1542-3. Foxe (v, pp. 463-464) gives the text, but only mentions one Proclamation, that of 1542-3.
[4] See the Six Articles Act (Gee and Hardy, *Documents*, p. 306) and the King's Book (*Formularies*, pp. 260-261).
[5] *A Potation* . . . (of Confession), P i, p. 100.
[6] ibid, P i, p. 101.
[7] ibid, P i, p. 102.

edition of his works, doubtless because they were still relevant
in view of the second Exhortation at the Communion, and the
Office for the Visitation of the Sick, in the Prayer Book.[1]
Comparison of the folio version of the *Potation* with the text
of the first edition of 1542, however, clearly shows the conservative character of the latter.[2]

Becon does his best to guard against misunderstanding.
Having shown that a Christian may pray anywhere, he
continues, against a marginal note, " Slander not, ye syco-
phants " :

> I have not spoken these things to make any person for to have
> the less devotion to go unto the church and accustomed place of
> prayer, when time requireth, (which thing God forbid that any
> man contrary to my meaning should gather of these my words,
> or thereby be occasioned the less to observe and keep the com-
> mendable order of this realm now-a-days used among us !) . . .[3]

Notwithstanding his own evident opinions, he warns against
an extreme view of justification by faith :

> Many in these our days glory much of the name of faith, and
> contend mainly that we are justified only and freely by faith,
> yea, and that without works. Let no man deceive himself . . .[4]

and at the beginning of the *Potation* a marginal note warns the
reader : " Slander not the author, that he teacheth faith
without good works".[5]

In conclusion, let us glance at the section in the conservative
Potation where Becon expounds the significance of the Lenten
ceremonies. It is worth comparing this with the King's Book,
and with the Rationale of ceremonies prepared by part of the
Commission which compiled that formulary.[6] First, Becon
describes the giving of ashes on Ash Wednesday, which

> . . . preacheth unto us, that we are nothing but ashes, dust, and
> earth, and to that we shall return again.[7]

---

[1] See F. E. Brightman, *The English Rite*, ii, pp. 673 and 828.

[2] See Detached Note E.

[3] *A New Pathway unto Prayer*, xxiv, P i, p. 159 ; *cf* Becon's views much
later, in *The Acts of Christ and of Antichrist*, II, Doctrine, §73, P iii, p. 533.

[4] *David's Harp* (second string), P i, p. 272.

[5] *A Potation* . . ., P i, p. 91.

[6] See Dixon, HCE, ii, pp. 311-313, and the note on p. 313. Strype, *Eccl.
Mem.*, I, i, p. 546, ascribes the Rationale or *Book of Ceremonies* to 1539, but
without sufficient reason ; Dixon suggests that it was never brought before
Convocation. It is printed in *Eccl. Mem.*, I, ii, pp. 411-433 (Appendix CIX).

[7] P i, p. 110.

This explanation is almost that of the King's Book ;[1]   the wording of the Rationale is different, but not the sense :

> . . . to put us in remembrance, in the beginning of Lent, of our frail nature, and the uncertainty of this life here.[2]

Next come the covering of the images and the veiling of the cross. The latter, says Becon, signifies

> . . . Christ the Son of God, which being promised of the Father to the Jews in the old law, was not then come, but only adumbrated, shadowed, and prefigured by certain types, figures, ceremonies . . . &c.[3]

Compare with this the Rationale, which speaks of the covering of both cross and images as signifying

> . . . not only the darkness of infidelity, which covered the face of the Jews in the Old Testament, but also the dark knowledg that they had of Christ . . . and the same is partly signified by the vail, which hid the secrets of sancta sanctorum from the people ; and in the time of Christ's passion was opened . . .[4]

Becon explains the covering of the images otherwise ; it shows men

> . . . that they that are sinners, and have a pleasure still therein to remain, are not worthy to behold the saints in heaven, which are represented by those images ; neither shall they at any time come unto that glory whereof the saints already have the fruition, except they repent them of their wicked living . . .

It also declares

> . . . the mourning and lamentation of sinners for their ungodly manners . . .

and, he characteristically points out, reminds us that

> . . . although we have in any part of the year past committed idolatry with [the images], yet at this time we should utterly give over this abomination, and only cleave to God and to his exceeding great mercy . . .[5]

While the Rationale and the King's Book give almost identical interpretations of the bearing of the palms,[6] Becon has a long and very interesting account of the ceremonies associated with the Palm Sunday processions, into the details of which we

---

[1] *Formularies*, p. 311.
[2] Strype, *Eccl. Mem.*, I, ii, p. 429.
[3] P i, p. 112.
[4] Strype, *Eccl. Mem.*, I, ii, p. 429.
[5] P i, p. 111.
[6] Strype, *Eccl. Mem.*, I, ii, p. 429 ; *Formularies*, p. 311.

cannot go here.[1] He then passes to the washing of the altars
on Maundy Thursday, which reminds us

> . . . how Christ washed his disciples' feet at his maundy, that we
> in like manner should be ready at all times to do good unto our
> christian brothers . . .[2]

The King's Book does not refer to this ceremony, but the
Rationale says it teaches that

> . . . we ought much more to prepare and wash our minds and
> consciences at al times ; and especially at this time, for the more
> worthy receiving of the . . . most high Sacrament.[3]

Becon makes no mention of the rest of the ceremonies explained
in the Rationale.

Nothing in this part of the *Potation* was omitted on revision,
but alterations were made to indicate that the ceremonies
described belonged to the times of superstition. It is interesting,
however, that in 1542 Becon seems not to have disapproved of
them ; otherwise he would hardly have explained them at such
length.

IV

Becon's early works have been considered in some detail,
partly because of their bearing upon his recantation and the
attitude of the authorities towards him, partly to enable his
position to be determined, and partly because of the light they
throw upon the method and policy behind his new manner of
teaching the people.

While there is no doubt that he had fully committed himself
to the protestant cause, his writings contain certain inconsistencies. In some respects his views are advanced, in others,
strictly orthodox. Occasionally his rhetoric seems to have
carried him further than he had intended or foreseen, and there
are ambiguities and contradictions which suggest that he had
not fully thought out his position. Enthusiasm for the Reformation, loyalty to his country, the king, and the supremacy,
attachment to many of the old ways, the over-boldness of self-
consequence and the timid circumspection of a sensitive

---

[1] The reader is referred to P i, pp. 112-116.
[2] P i, p. 116.
[3] Strype, *Eccl. Mem.*, I, ii, p. 431.

character, all combine to make him appear at once decided and undecided.

But these apparent inconsistencies are more than an indication of Becon's character and position at this time. They tend to confirm the probability that his retirement into Kent was part of a scheme to enable him to continue as a writer the services which he had hitherto rendered to the protestant cause as a preacher. To produce eleven treatises and one long preface in two years was no mean achievement, but none of these works makes any original contribution to the *corpus* of reformation theology. Instead, arguments are brought to a conclusion, or a case is built up, simply by proceeding from one assertion, with its appropriate biblical or patristic proof, to another. Each composition is a piece of propaganda designed to establish the protestant case, and must be approached as propaganda.

This immediately gives a clue to the moderate and orthodox features of his writing. Becon's aim was to supply a continuous stream of literature inculcating and expounding the views of the reformers, yet sufficiently uncontroversial and temperate to avoid exciting unwelcome attentions. Hence he refrains from any but the most innocuous allusions to the Mass and the Blessed Sacrament, for otherwise he would come under the condemnation of the Six Articles. Hence his conservative attitude to ceremonies and auricular confession, and his insistence upon the lawfulness of the royal supremacy and the duty of obedience to the king and the magistrates. Hence, too, his fervent professions of patriotism, his denunciations of Papists, Anabaptists, and all who imperil the safety or well-being of the state, and his anxiety not to be misunderstood and misrepresented. His readers, and still more, the authorities, must know him for a true Englishman, an advocate of toleration in so far as it may be expedient, and a loyal citizen and churchman. And under cover of these disarming protestations he introduces his propaganda. His object was not to expound or defend the great doctrines of the Reformation, but to accustom his readers to the protestant viewpoint and terminology by a process of insinuation and repetition—a device not unknown in our own day. His recantation shows that he did

not always succeed in keeping within the bounds of moderation
—indeed, that was impossible in the nature of the case. And
it is impossible always to say whether his moderation is
genuine, or simply due to uncertainty, perplexity, or deliberate
suppression. But there is evidence enough to suggest that his
plan, possibly even his orders, required the method of moderation. By evading suspicion as far as possible, his object was
to keep the teaching of the Reformers before the people during
the catholic reaction, and to encourage perseverance in times
of trial, thus preparing for the anticipated turn of the tide in
favour of the protestant cause.

There is no reason to think that Becon's activity formed
part of any extensive or concerted " underground " campaign.
Nothing leads us to suspect the existence of such a movement.
But there is every indication of an isolated and, as it happened,
short-lived experiment in protestant propaganda conducted by
a young and fluent writer supported, and perhaps directed, by
a small group of gentry who sought to further the Reformation
in England.

Precautions and subterfuges were unavailing. Theodore
Basille could no more elude the vigilance of the Privy Council
and its agents than could Thomas Becon. The new author's
works, pouring from the press of a notorious " sacramentary",
soon aroused suspicions which investigations in Kent confirmed
—and so, with apprehension, examination, and recantation for
the second time, there closed yet another chapter in the life of
the young reformer.

CHAPTER V

WANDERINGS IN THE MIDLANDS
1543-1547

I

W HEN Dr. H. E. Jacobs said that Becon's career
showed "great weakness and vacillation in the presence
of danger",[1] he was thinking, presumably, of his two
recantations, his "lurking" in Kent, his flight into the
Midlands, and his "skulking" and eventual escape to the
Continent in 1553. But before endorsing this charge of
cowardice we must enquire whether such an estimate of his
conduct does Becon full justice.

In the matter of recantation it is interesting to compare
Becon with Wisdom. Becon seems to have had no remorse or
scruples of conscience about either of his submissions, but the
one which Wisdom made in 1543 so weighed upon his mind
that he composed a full retraction in which he admitted that
he had committed this "impiety" through fear of death.[2]
It was not like Becon to make such confessions, but his apparent
indifference to what was, for Wisdom, an ignominious lapse, a
"great slander and occasion of evil . . . committed against the
congregation of God", cannot be explained simply in terms of
pride and anxiety to save face. Nor would concealment gain
anything, for all knew who had recanted and who had not;

---

[1] *The Lutheran Movement in England*, p. 324.
[2] See Foxe, v, App. XXII* ; the revocation in full may be found in a
collection of *Letters of the Martyrs* in the possession of Emanuel College,
Cambridge, vol. ii, foll. 88-130. In writing about Wisdom's revocation, Becon
conceals the fact that his friend had recanted, and refers to his "confutation
of those errors which were imputed and laid to his charge very unjustly of his
adversaries, a book farced with all kind of godly learning" (*The Jewel of Joy*,
P ii, p. 423), and not to "that shameful bill that Winchester devised".

yet Becon's two submissions were never held against him. Foxe, indeed, passes them over as of little account :

> What should we say to Maister Beacon, who, although he recanted with other in king Henry's time, yet, in queen Mary's days, how hardly escaped he with his life . . . ! The like is to be said of M. Wisdome . . . [and several others] . . . ; which all recanted in king Henry's time, and yet good soldiers after in the church of Christ.[1]

Maitland has two essays on the subject of Puritan veracity in which he shows that

> . . . it was considered not only allowable, but meritorious, to tell lies for the sake of the good cause in which they were engaged . . . they did not hesitate . . . with great deliberation and solemnity, to state what they knew to be false . . .[2]

He does not suggest that this expedient of mendacity was employed extensively, but it could clearly have its uses in persecution. Does it explain the difference between the attitudes of the two friends to their submissions ? Did Wisdom's recantation cost him such distress of spirit, while Becon's occasioned neither self-reproach nor censure, simply because the former was assumed to be genuine (that is, an act of apostasy), and therefore required a convincing apology, whereas the latter was known to be deliberately false, and so excited no concern ? If Becon was in some sense an " official " propagandist, it may well have been understood that should he get into trouble, no questions would be asked as to his manner of extricating himself. As a martyr he would have been of little value to the protestant cause ; alive, he had proved usefulness and great potentialities. If he came into collision with the authorities, a way of escape lay to hand ; a recantation, if plausible enough, would satisfy the Council and the Henricians without deceiving Becon's own party. His submission has a flamboyant style ; is it fanciful also to detect a note of insincerity, and even of satisfaction in a successful piece of deception ? The question must remain open, for the evidence is insufficient to warrant any final conclusion, but I suspect that Becon's second recantation at any rate was false, and cannot be attributed to " weakness and vacillation in the presence of danger".

[1] Foxe, v, p. 696.
[2] *Essays on Subjects connected with the Reformation in England*, pp. 1-2.

E

May not this be true also of his retirements into Kent and the Midlands ? So long as it involved no compromise on principles, evasion of persecution was usually considered legitimate. Ridley,[1] Cranmer,[2] and Sandys,[3] among others, affirm the " godly wisdom " of withdrawal from the malice of the enemy, for which they claim the licence of Christ himself.[4] By similar arguments Becon also justifies his decision to seek a retreat where he might be free from molestation :

> . . . when neither by speaking nor by writing I could do good, I thought it best not rashly to throw myself into the ravening paws of these greedy wolves, but for a certain space to absent myself from their tyranny according to the doctrine of the gospel.
>
> For as there is " a time to speak", so there is " a time to keep silence". When the poor are oppressed and trodden under the foot, then " shall the wise man," saith the prophet, " hold his peace ; for the time is evil." And we have a manifest command of our Saviour Christ, that we should " not give that which is holy unto dogs, nor cast pearls before swine, lest they tread them under their feet, and they turn again and all-to rent " us . . .
>
> Where things be so ordered that the truth can bear no place, nor the professors thereof be thankfully received, but rather blasphemed, persecuted, imprisoned, and ungently handled ; what should men do but shake off the dust of their feet, for a witness against them at the day of judgement, and depart unto some other place, where they may do good, as Christ and the apostles did, and quietly to abide the pleasure of God . . .[5]

If Becon was weak and vacillating, so also were so many of his contemporaries, protestant and catholic, humble and distinguished alike, that Dr. Jacobs' charge loses all its force in an individual case. A different interpretation of Becon's conduct is possible if his recantations are attributed to policy and his retirements into Kent and Derbyshire to prudence.

II

The story of the next three years can be told for the most part in Becon's own words.[6] Quitting London, we may suppose,

[1] *A Pituous Lamentation of the Miserable Estate of the Churche of Christ in Englande, Works* (PS), pp. 62 and 65, marginal note.
[2] Letter cccxi, *Works* (PS), ii, p. 445.
[3] *Sermons* (PS), xvii, p. 335.
[4] See Matt. x. 23.
[5] *The Jewel of Joy*, P ii, pp. 419-420.
[6] ibid, P ii, pp. 420-427.

very soon after 8th July, 1543, he made his way into Norfolk, where he does not seem to have delayed.

> After I . . . had taken my leave of my most sweet mother, and of my other dear friends, I travelled into Derbyshire, and from thence into the Peak, whither I appointed my books and clothes to be brought.
> *Eusebius* : Into the Peak ? Lord God, what made you there ? That is a marvellous and a barren country, and, as it is thought, such a country that neither hath learning, nor yet no spark of godliness.[1]
> *Philemon* : Mine intent was, by exercising the office of a schoolmaster, to engraft Christ and the knowledge of him in the breasts of those scholars whom God should appoint unto me for to be taught.

Becon's itinerary is not clear, but he probably entered Derbyshire from the south-east and struck across it in the direction of north Staffordshire, encountering as he approached the boundary the broken high land around Dovedale. Among these hills he found sanctuary for a time :

> Coming into a little village, called Alsop in the Dale, I chanced upon a certain gentleman called Alsop,[2] lord of that village, a man not only ancient in years, but also ripe in the knowledge of Christ's doctrine. . . . After we had saluted one another and taken a sufficient repast for that present, he shewed me certain books which he called his jewels and principal treasures. . . . there was the new testament, after the translation of . . . Myles Coverdale, which seemed to be as well worn by the diligent reading thereof as ever was any portass or mass-book among the papists. . . . he had many other godly books . . . [including] . . . all the books published in the name of Thomas Becon[3] . . . In these godly treatises this ancient gentleman among the mountains and rocks occupied himself both diligently and virtuously.

Becon remained at Alsop in the Dale, in the mansion standing north-west of the church on an eminence which commanded the dale and the surrounding hills,[4] until news arrived which caused him to leave Derbyshire :

[1] That is, reformed teaching.

[2] Probably John Alsop, son of Thomas Alsop and —Erdeswick of Sandon, Staffs.; see the pedigree of Alsop in S. Glover, *History of the County of Derby*, vol. ii.

[3] It is curious that Becon should make this statement, since all his works published up to this time had borne the name Theodore Basille.

[4] Glover, *op. cit.*, ii, p. 20.

> . . . I learned that R. Wisdom was in Staffordshire . . . He was
> the same to me that Aristarchus was to Paul.[1] Desiring greatly
> to see him I bade my friends in the Peak farewell, and made
> haste toward him. . . . I found him in the house of a certain
> faithful brother, called John Olde. . . . He was to us as Jason
> was to Paul and Silas. He received us joyfully into his house, and
> liberally, for the Lord's sake, ministered all good things to our
> necessities. . . . After that we had passed over certain days in
> the house of that most loving brother . . . I know not of what
> friend our dear brother Robert Wisdom was called away by
> letters, which was to us both no small pain and grief.

After his friend's departure Becon turned again to his
tutorial work ; not improbably he and Olde, whom Strype calls
a " teacher of youth as well as of the gospel",[2] ran a school
together, and he professes himself well satisfied with the
results of his instruction.

Becon took good note of the manners and religion of the
people in the parts where he travelled. In the Peak

> . . . all their religion consisted in hearing matins and mass, in
> superstitious worshipping of saints, in hiring soul-carriers to sing
> trentals, in pattering upon beads, and in such other popish
> pedlary.

They stood in strong contrast to the " ancient gentleman
among the mountains and rocks", whose devotion to the
scriptures seemed the more astonishing since in those parts
Christ had never been truly preached ; the wilds of Derbyshire
had scarcely felt the impact of the Reformation. The ignorance
of the common people was hardly remarkable, for " the priests
in that country are very basely learned". Yet Becon confesses
that

> The people where I have travelled for the most part are reason-
> able and quiet enough, yea, and very conformable to God's truth.
> If any be stubbornly obstinate, it is for fault of knowledge, and
> because they have been seduced of blind guides.

In Staffordshire he found them

> . . . not altogether unlike the people of the Peak, but that they
> were not in all points commonly so superstitious ; they savoured
> somewhat more of pure religion. This, I think, came to pass
> through certain English books that were among them, and
> through travellers to and fro London.

---

[1] Does this imply that Becon and Wisdom had been in prison together
(cf Col. iv. 10), or simply that they had been persecuted together ?
[2] Eccl. Mem., II, ii, p. 47.

The priests, however, were

> . . . all massmongers, applying their portass and mass-book very diligently, but the holy bible very little.
>
> . . . they are not such priests, as whose " lips keep knowledge", neither can their " mouth utter the law of God", if any man should require it of them.

Nor were the clergy of the Midlands exceptional, as " the childish ignorance that was found in priests at the king's majesty's visitation "[1] proved.

In 1545 John Olde was presented to the living of Cubbington, a village some two miles outside Leamington in Warwickshire ; thither he repaired, and Becon soon followed him.

> After that I had consumed a year in that country [Stafford-shire] and somewhat more in the virtuous education and godly bringing up of youth, I departed into Warwickshire, where in like manner as afore I freely enjoyed the liberality of my most sweet and dear friend John Olde. . . . There likewise taught I divers gentlemen's sons . . .[2]

Of all the places into which his travels took him, Becon declares that " Warwickshire was to me most dear and pleasant", for it " ministered unto me the acquaintance and friendship of many learned men". Foremost among these was Latimer, whom he had admired when a student at Cambridge. Some twenty miles north of Cubbington lay the small village of Baxterley, where John Glover, " a man of primitive piety", dwelt in a " fair mansion " which he had built.[3] To Baxterley Hall Latimer was a frequent visitor, and Becon probably met him there several times. Others came to see Glover,

> . . . whereof some were men of worship well bent toward the holy scriptures, some were men very godly learned in the laws of the Most Highest, and professors of the same. So oft as I was in their company, methought I was clean delivered from Egypt and

---

[1] Doubtless the first Edwardine Visitation of 1547, see Dixon, HCE, ii, pp. 430 ff. The ignorance revealed by Hooper's Visitation in 1552 shows that things were little better five years later in Gloucester diocese ; see below, p. 59 ; also Dixon, HCE, iii, pp. 462-463, and the *English Historical Review*, xix (1904), pp. 98 ff.

[2] Among them, perhaps, was Basil Feilding, to whom Becon dedicated *The Sick Man's Salve*, and who married Godith Willington of Barcheston in south Warwickshire.

[3] See R. Demaus, *Hugh Latimer*, p. 468.

quietly placed in the new Jerusalem . . . ; so sweet a thing is it
to be in the company of godly learned men.[1]

Becon also spent some time in Leicestershire, where he
" had familiarity only with one learned man, a countryman of
ours [a Norfolk man], called John Aylmer", then living as a
tutor at Bradgate, the seat of the Marquis of Dorset.[2] It is
impossible to tell whether this meeting occurred during 1543,
when Becon may have called at Bradgate on his way into
Derbyshire, or whether he crossed into Leicestershire from
Baxterley. The latter seems the more likely.[3]

Late in 1546 Becon had to leave his pleasant retreat :

> . . . behold, unlooked for, were letters sent unto me from my most
> dear mother, in which she required me to return to my native
> country, and to be a staff of her old age ; forasmuch as my
> father-in-law[4] was departed from this vale of misery. . . .
> immediately after, not without the friendly consent of my well-
> willers, [I] departed from Warwickshire, and with all haste
> repaired home.

So ends the account of his wanderings in the Midlands.

III

Before his return to Norfolk, a proclamation dated 8th July,
1546, against " such Englyshe bookes as conteyne pernicious
and detestable errours and heresies "[5] had proscribed a large
number of works " infected with false opinions", including
thirteen[6] by " Theodore Basille, alias Thomas Becon". The

---

[1] Mullinger, op. cit., i, p. 574, erroneously supposes that this passage
relates to the meetings of Cambridge reformers in the White Horse Inn for
the study and discussion of Luther's works. Becon was not at the University
then.

[2] On Bradgate, and Becon's visit, see Nichol's Leicestershire, III, ii,
pp. 661-680.

[3] Brook, Lives of the Puritans, i, pp. 167-168, says that from Staffordshire
Becon moved into Leicestershire, and thence into Warwickshire, but he gives
no authority for this statement.

[4] i.e., step-father.

[5] Foxe, v, p. 838. See also L & P. Henry VIII, xxi, pt. 1, No. 1233, p. 611.
This item is calendared by mistake, from an undated draft, in L & P. Henry
VIII, xvii (1542), No. 177, p. 79 : see also Foxe, v, pp. 565-568.

[6] In Bib. I, Nos. 13, 9, 10, 2, 3, 7a-c, 4, 14, 5, 7, 11, 6, and 12, set out in
this order.

list did not include one book, written shortly before or after
Becon's second recantation,

> . . . even in the bloody boisterous burning time, when the reading
> of the holy bible . . . was forbidden the poor lay people . . .[1]

and published anonymously.   This was *The Governance of
Virtue*, a directory of the Christian life consisting mainly of
sentences and examples from scripture, put forth with the
avowed object of familiarizing the " simple and unlearned "
folk with the Bible they were not allowed to possess or read.
It proved a popular work,

> . . . greatly desired and greedily read almost of all men . . . as the
> often printing of the book doth right well declare.

Becon prepared a revised edition in 1550,[2] and several others
were issued during the next fifty years.

Becon's pen was not idle during his sojourn in the Midlands.
He wrote two works in very poor verse, *A Dialogue of Christ's
Nativity between the Angel and the Shepherds* and *An Invective
against Whoredom*,[3] and there were several compositions
belonging to this period, the titles of which we do not know,
still in manuscript when *The Jewel of Joy* was written. Becon
also translated from Latin " divers little treatises", the originals
of which I cannot trace ; they were probably by continental
reformers.   Only one is extant, *The Solace of the Soul*, a
devotional work offering Christian comfort to those in sickness
and adversity.   Another, *The Commendation of Death*, may have
been the first version of *The Praise of Death*, a dialogue between
Man and Reason which appeared in the folio edition. A third,
The Shield of Salvation, was also probably devotional in
character.

---

[1] *The Jewel of Joy*, P i, p. 399. Becon wrote *The Jewel* in 1550, as far as
we know, and says, just before the passage quoted, that *The Governance of
Virtue* had been composed " about eight years past " ; 1542, however, is too
early a date.

[2] See P i, pp. 399-400.

[3] Neither of these works is printed in the PS edition ; the *Invective*
begins :

> Downe with the whoredom of Englande
> which hath this realme so lõge made bonde ;
> Down with hyr whelpes that are so fonde,
> Let them al go down a down a.

> (see F ii, fol. cclxxxxii recto).

CHAPTER VI

THE PROTESTANT ASCENDANCY, 1547-1553

I

UPON the accession of Edward VI, Thomas Becon was one of those who gained the reward of their attachment to the Reformation during the late reign. The notice excited by his writings, and the interest of friends like Latimer and Olde, and patrons like Wentworth,[1] were no doubt instrumental in procuring him a chaplaincy in the household of the Lord Protector, though we do not know exactly when he took up his duties.

Two of Somerset's family received in due course the customary recompense of patronage ; to the Lady Jane Seymour was dedicated the revised *Governance of Virtue*, which appeared in 1550, and to the Duchess Anne, *The Flower of Godly Prayers*, in acknowledgment of her liberality most bounteously shown to the author since his first entering her service.[2]

The latter work contains two prayers, one " For a faithful man being in trouble or endurance", and the other " A thanksgiving for his deliverance",[3] which were composed during the period of Somerset's first disgrace. Minor alterations, such as the substitution of " our faithful brother " for " our lord and master", adapted them for general use, but the prayers can be found in their original form appended to *The Spiritual and most precious Pearl*, a book published in 1550. They are entitled

A humble peticyon to the lord, practysed in the commune prayer of the whole famylye at Shene, during the trouble of their lord and master the duke of Somerset his grace ; gathered

[1] Latimer had secured for Olde the living of Cubbington, which was in the gift of the Duchess of Somerset, then Countess of Hertford, and Wentworth and Somerset were cousins.
[2] Preface, P iii, p. 13.
[3] P iii, pp. 34-36.

54

and set furth by Thomas Becon, minister there. Which trouble began the VI of October the year of our Lord MD. XLIX and ended the VI of Febuarye then next ensuing.

Becon probably refers to this anxious time in his preface to the revised *Governance of Virtue* :

> Certain weeks past, considering the miserable face of this too much wretched and lamentable world, and weighing with myself that the next and most ready way to redress our miseries is to fly unto God with continual and hearty prayer, I made a book entitled " The Flower of Godly Prayers " . . .[1]

and in the preface to the latter, apprehensive of the consequences of his patron's misfortunes, he exclaims, " fortune goeth forth forwardly to frown upon me."[2] Nevertheless he survived the ultimate fall of the Protector without being prejudiced, so far as we can judge, by his connexion with him.

With these two works may be mentioned *The Pomander of Prayer*, dedicated to Anne of Cleves. It is not known when this was written or published, but it later ran into several editions. The esteem in which Becon's devotional manuals were held is shown by the fact that out of the fifty-three " godly prayers for divers purposes " and " general prayers " included in the Primer of 1553 no less than forty-three are drawn from the *Flower* and the *Pomander*.[3]

II

Becon also received preferment at the hands of Cranmer himself, being appointed one of the six Preachers at Canter-

---

[1] P i, p. 399.

[2] P iii, p. 12. Becon makes a similar alliterative complaint in the preface to the *Fortress of the Faithful*, with reference to his poverty, P ii, p. 592.

[3] Ten are taken from the *Flower* almost as they stand ; one, " For Bishops and Ministers of God's Word", gains greatly by drastic abbreviation (see P iii, pp. 21-24, and *Liturgies of Edward VI* (PS), pp. 456-457). Becon's prayers will be found in the latter, pp. 454-476, the remaining thirty-two coming from the *Pomander*. Churton, *Life of Nowell*, p. 21, n., says : " Wharton's Dream in this same year 1578 . . . in the address to the Reader, complaining of the use of improper books, says, ' They will have their Palace of Pleasure, the wanton Epistle of Ovid, the bowget of Merry Demaundes ; ——fewe or none will have maister Becon's sweete Pomander to smell to.' "

bury.[1] The Archbishop also made him one of his chaplains,[2] and invited him to contribute to the Book of Homilies, then in preparation. For this Becon wrote the homily " against Whoredom and Uncleanness", generally known as the Homily against Adultery,[3] a sin he often denounced in his writings.

The beginning of the reign was marked by an attempt to control preaching. On 6th February, 1547-8, a proclamation limited to their own cures all preachers other than the diocesan, the Archbishop of Canterbury, one of the king's Visitors, and those holding the royal licence.[4] This was followed on 24th April, 1548, by another, depriving parish priests of the right to preach in their own churches.[5] On 13th May the licensed preachers themselves received an admonition,[6] and finally, on 23rd September, all licences were withdrawn until the passing of the Act of Uniformity. Eighty licensed preachers are enumerated in a list of the names of " certain persons that have had license to preach under Ecclesiastical seal since July in anno 1547",[7] and among them is one *Thomas Beaton.* Since this name does not recur in contemporary records, there can be little doubt that the reference is actually to Thomas Becon, or Beacon, as it was sometimes spelt ; a slip of the pen would easily account for the error.[8] In favour of this presumption

---

[1] The others were Nicholas and Lancelot Ridley, Richard Turner, Richard Beaseley, and John Joseph. Strype says, " These converted not a few to sincere religion ; as may appear by those numbers of Canterbury that in Queen Mary's reign suffered the torment of fire for their profession of the Gospel " (*Cranmer*, i, p. 229). On the six Preachers see also Strype, *Eccl. Mem.*, I, ii, pp. 406-407 ; Burnet, *Reformation*, iii, p. 253 and vi, pp. 228-229 (the Canterbury scheme) ; Dixon, HCE, ii, pp. 221-225.

[2] Strype, *Cranmer*, i, p. 607 ; Jacobs, *op. cit.*, p. 324, gives the date of Becon's appointment as 24th March, 1547 (? 1546-7), but states no authority for this, and I have not been able to confirm it. He has no doubt confused the chaplaincy with the rectory of St. Stephen's, Walbrook, to which Becon was presented on this date.

[3] P ii, pp. 643-650 ; *Homilies*, pp. 123-140. In 1549 this homily was divided into three parts, introductions connecting each part with that last read.

[4] See Strype, *Eccl. Mem.*, II, ii, pp. 347-348 ; Burnet, *Reformation*, v, pp. 188-190.

[5] See Dixon, HCE, ii, p. 530 and Burnet, *Reformation*, v, p. 193, n. 86. The priests were said, among other things, to have encouraged the idea that for every baptism, marriage, and burial half a crown would be exacted.

[6] See Burnet, *Reformation*, v, pp. 193-196.

[7] *State Papers* (Domestic), Edward VI, x, pt. ii, No. 34 ; Dixon, HCE, ii, pp. 485-486, n.

[8] There is no doubt that the spelling in the original document is "Beaton". See also p. 93 below for another instance of this spelling of Becon's name.

there is Becon's reputation as a preacher, enhanced by his appointment at Canterbury, and his standing at this time with the Primate and the Protector; also, his defence of the preachers in the *Fortress of the Faithful* and elsewhere is suggestive.[1]

We hear nothing of Becon's preaching activities, but no doubt his time was chiefly occupied in the service of Cranmer and, until his fall, of Somerset, as well as in unceasing literary labour. To his other duties were added also those of parish priest, for on 24th March, 1547-8, he was presented by the Grocers' Company to the living of St. Stephen, Walbrook, in the City of London.[2]

III

During the sitting of the Convocation which assembled on 5th November, 1547, clerical marriage was discussed, and Becon records a conversation on the subject which took place at that time :

> . . . sittinge at the table of the moste reuerende Father in God Thomas Cranmere (. . . sometime my Lorde and Master and moste beneficyall Patrone and mayntayner of my studyes[3] . . .) . . . I hearde the matter of the marryage of Pryestes was there in dysputacyon verye learnedly and soberly debated ; some alledging what the aduersaryes had to obiecte in this behalfe, some answerynge and confutinge all the obiectyons, prouinge them worthy rather the nam of abiectyons than obiectyons. At the laste commynge unto the vowe . . . I harde Doctour Redman, Doctoure Haynes, Doctoure Tonge, Doctoure Taylour afterwarde Byshoppe of Lyncolne, with dyuers other learned men, whyche at that tyme were presente affyrme and saye, yea and that not wythoute probable argumentes and reasons, that the Pryestes of Englande are not votoryes, nor bounde with any vowe of single life, but that they maye frely and with good conscience marry . . .[4]

---

[1] See below, pp. 65-67.

[2] Hennessy, *Nov. Repert.*, p. 386 : " Thomas Bekon, 1547-8, Mch. 24th." ; also Newcourt, *Repertorium*, i, p. 540.

[3] In the preface-dedicatory to *A . . . Treatise of Fasting* Becon also speaks of " the thankfulness of my heart toward your most honourable lordship [Cranmer], for the manifold benefits which ye have bounteously bestowed upon me . . .", P ii, p. 527.

[4] *The Book of Matrimony*, F i, fol. DCvi recto and verso.

On 17th December, in the eighth session of Convocation, a proposal was made to abolish all canons, laws, and customs which forbade the marriage of priests and religious. It was carried by fifty-three votes to twenty-two, and among those who supported it were two who had taken part in the discussion at Cranmer's table—Dr. Taylor and Dr. Redman.[1] The measure was passed by the Commons in a modified form, permitting, not the marriage of priests, but the ordination of married men ; it reached the Lords, however, too late to be dealt with before the end of the session. Clerical marriage, without restrictions or conditions, was finally legalized in 1549.

IV

Becon's works written at this time present an interesting picture of the state of the country, as seen through the eyes of one of the dominant party.

He celebrates with enthusiasm the triumph of the Reformation,[2] recounting the benefits which the Church had received through this last and most merciful visitation of God,[3] and the Divine vengeance which had overtaken those who heeded not the preaching of the martyrs and confessors of the last reign. Yet all is not well ; there are reactionaries who long for the Henrician flesh-pots and despise the pure protestant manna, and there are time-servers and " gross gospellers " who

> . . . have the holy scriptures swimming in their lips, and God's book either in their hands or hanging at their girdles,

while all the time denying the Gospel in their lives, being only " stout disciples of Christ so long as Christ feedeth them with bread". The " disobedience and stubborn papists " still remain, resisting God's word " maliciously and of a set purpose", while " anabaptists, Davidians, libertines, and such other pestilent

---

[1] Redman did not actually vote with the majority, but being " in such great credit universally for his ability in deciding questions of conscience", was asked to give his opinion, which Strype prints in *Cranmer*, i, p. 223. This contains, no doubt, the substance of Redman's argument at the Archbishop's table.

[2] See *The Flower of Godly Prayers*, P iii, pp. 4 and 65-68, and *The Jewel of Joy*, P ii, p. 415.

[3] See *The Flower of Godly Prayers*, P iii, p. 11.

sects " sow " wicked and ungodly opinions " in the hearts of the people.[1] And to all these must be added the impious, the licentious, and the evil-living, before whose eyes there is no fear of God.

Unless these abuses are removed, Becon prophesies that God will allow the work of the Reformation to be undone, and popish superstition and civil tyranny will return.[2] Indeed, a similar judgment had already been executed for all to see. The imperial victory in the Schmalkald war, and the ensuing Interim, had proved a great setback to the Lutherans, and preachers and divines who felt that their cause was almost lost in Germany were seeking refuge in England.[3] He does not fail to point the moral accordingly.

The clergy also come in for castigation. Pluralism is rife, teaching and hospitality are neglected,[4] and the " christian and godly preachers " who attempt to supply what is wanting in the ministry of the Word are despised and set at nought.[5] The state of affairs revealed by the royal visitation of 1547 and Hooper's diocesan visitation of 1551,[6] shows that Becon's criticism was fully warranted. Nor was it only the older clergy who were to blame, for Northumberland, in January, 1552, directed a scathing indictment against the men " that the king's

[1] See ibid, pp. 5-6 and P ii, p. 415 ; also Hooper's letter to Bullinger, *Orig. Let.* XXXIII (i, pp. 65-66), Dixon, HCE, iii, pp. 472-473 (the Davidians in Kent), and *The Political History of England*, vi (Pollard), p. 68. Froude, *History of England*, v, p. 19, seems to consider that Becon's denunciation in *The Jewel of Joy* (P ii, p. 415) refers, not to the sectaries, but to extremists among the reformers, men such as Ponet and Hooper, and especially Northumberland, " of this class of men the highest living representative". He bestows upon him in consequence the epithet " large-minded "—presumably for condemning the vices of men whose faults he might have been expected to pass over, since they were furthering the cause to which he had lent his own support. But Froude is in error here, for the passage in question was written at the beginning of Edward's reign, and can be paralleled from Becon's early works. It is not always easy to decide whether Becon means by " gospellers " the hypocritical and time-serving professors of reformed principles, or the religious radicals and sectaries who exhibited not only heretical but also antinomian tendencies. But it is certain that he cannot have meant such as Hooper and Ponet.

[2] Preface, *The Flower of Godly Prayers*, P iii, p. 12 ; *cf* an earlier prediction of similar import in the prologue to *News out of Heaven*, P i, p. 39.

[3] Preface, *The Flower of Godly Prayers*, P iii, p. 10.

[4] Preface, *The Fortress of the Faithful*, P ii, p. 587 ; *cf The Jewel of Joy*, P ii, pp. 431-432.

[5] *The Fortress of the Faithful*, P ii, p. 611.

[6] See above, p. 51.

majesty hath of late preferred "—many of them in high position in the Church.[1] But Bernard Gilpin, who had deserted the Old Learning to become one of the most formidable champions of the New, pointed out in a sermon preached at Court that clerical ignorance and neglect were often due to the rapacity of unscrupulous patrons who preferred unlettered men and even thrust benefices upon retainers in order to secure the revenues of the benefice.[2] Unfortunately the king, " upon some occasion detained", was not there to hear him.

In *The Jewel of Joy* Becon put forward some " counsel worthy to be followed " in the matter of Church reform. He suggests the appointment of " learned curates " in every parish, and if this should prove impossible, the provision of a local itinerant ministry of " learned and godly preachers". He continues :

> And *let the other priests be ministers under the superintendents, or overseers*, and in their absence read to the people the . . . scriptures, and the homilies, reverently minister the sacraments, visit the sick people, make collections for the poor, and virtuously bring up the youth of the town . . .[3]

This counsel did not move the young Josiah and his advisers, but it may have prompted Hooper to appoint certain clergy in his own diocese, with the title of Superintendent, to oversee the rest.[4] This would not be difficult to carry into effect, but to the provision of competent parish priests there were other obstacles than the irresponsibility and covetousness of patrons —and chief among them was the fact that the " learned curates " were no longer to be had.

When Becon was at Cambridge the universities were thronged with poor scholars like himself, and it was generally from the ranks of the small tenants and yeomen that the learned or educated classes were recruited. Not the least important consequence of the Dissolution was that thereafter

---

[1] *Political History of England*, vi (Pollard), p. 73.

[2] See Strype, *Eccl. Mem.*, II, ii, pp. 25-29, and Dixon, HCE, iii, pp. 533-534 and references.

[3] P ii, p. 422, my italics.

[4] See Dixon, HCE, iii, p. 452. It is difficult, as Dixon points out, to understand Hooper's innovation (or, for that matter, Becon's suggestion) when there were archdeacons at hand and the importance of the rural deans could have been revived.

the sons of the gentry and nobility, who had formerly acquired
their sufficiency of learning in the schools attached to the great
monastic houses, began increasingly to resort to Oxford and
Cambridge, taking not only the room but often the scholarships
and exhibitions intended for the sons of the poor.   Both
learning and the places where it had flourished fell into
contempt, and divinity in particular was neglected.[1]   Becon
shows himself fully aware of the gravity of the situation, and
in *The Sick Man's Salve* he commends the plight of the poor
scholar to the generosity of testators by the example of the
dying *Epaphroditus*, who leaves £100 to each of the Universities.[2]

V

The manners, the social unrest, and the economic chaos of
the time are also reflected in Becon's writings.

After denouncing the building of " gorgeous houses and
sumptuous mansions" (a bold step, when his own patron
himself, by ruthless acts of sacrilege, had reared in the Strand
the magnificent palace of Somerset House) he goes on to
condemn those who give their time to pleasure and banqueting,[3]
and holds up to ridicule " the vain and foolish light apparel "
favoured by the idle and wealthy :

> Neither with fine clothe, nor with satin, damask, velvet, nor
> with cloth of gold, did God apparel Adam, neither did he trim and
> set forth our grandmother Eve with sumptuous apparel of cloth
> of silver, or cloth of gold, neither did he set upon her head a
> French hood with an edge of gold, besides pearls and precious
> stones, and such other trim-trams, I cannot tell what. . . . I
> think no realm in the world, no, not among the Turks and
> Saracens, doth so much in the vanity of their apparel, as the
> Englishmen do at this present. Their coat must be made after
> the Italian fashion, their cloak after the use of the Spaniards,
> their gown after the manner of the Turks ; and at the last their
> dagger must be Scottish, with a Venetian tassel of silk. I speak
> nothing of their doubtlets and hoses, which for the most part
> are so minced, cut, and jagged, that shortly after they become
> both torn and ragged.

[1] See Latimer, *Sermons* (PS), pp. 178-179 ; Strype, *Cranmer*, i, p. 242
and *Eccl. Mem.*, II, ii, p. 29 ; *Orig. Let.*, ii, p. 710.

[2] See P iii, pp. 118-119.

[3] *The Jewel of Joy*, P ii, pp. 435 and 440-441.

He dismisses more shortly the

> . . . light and wanton apparel of women . . . partly because it is
> so monstruous, and partly because I have not been nor yet am
> very much acquainted with them, whereby I might be the more
> able to describe their proud peacock's tails . . .[1]

But he does not omit to exclaim against their " flaring out and
colouring of their hair " and " painting of their faces".

For many of the new nobility and gentry he has nothing
good to say :

> . . . they are such as this common proverb noteth :
> > As riseth my good,
> > So riseth my blood.
>
> They think all nobility to consist in the abundance of worldly
> goods, in wearing of golden chains and costly apparel, in having
> fair houses and pleasant gardens. . . . they move every stone, as
> they say, to maintain and set forth their unnoble nobility, not
> caring how they come by it, so that they have it. All is fish that
> cometh to the net : it is good to be taking. *Bonus est odor lucri
> ex re qualibet.*[2]

But he does not despise the *parvenu* more than the man of
noble birth and " base and vile manners", for " The true
nobility consisteth . . . in the suppressing of vice and embracing
of virtue".[3] And concerning good and bad alike the times had
taught one sobering truth :

> . . . he which is this day a lord highly in favour, and a man of
> great possessions, is to-morrow a traitor, and not worth a gally
> half-penny.[4]

But Becon reserves his severest rebukes for those whose
relentless policy of enclosure had precipitated the agrarian
crisis, and had caused so much distress among the agricultural
population :

> . . . the cause of all this wretchedness and beggary in the common-
> weal are the greedy gentlemen, which are sheepmongers and
> graziers. . . . Since they began to be sheep-masters and feeders of
> cattle, we neither had victual nor cloth of any reasonable price.
> No marvel ; for these forestallers of the market . . . have gotten
> all things so into their hands, that the poor man must either buy

---

[1] *The Jewel of Joy*, P ii, pp. 438-439.
[2] *The Fortress of the Faithful*, P ii, p. 499.
[3] *The Jewel of Joy*, P ii, p. 436.
[4] ibid, P ii, p. 435.

it at their price, or else miserably starve for hunger, and wretchedly die for cold : for they are touched with no pity toward the poor.[1]

How join they lordship to lordship, manor to manor, farm to farm, land to land, pasture to pasture, house to house, and house for a vantage ! How do the rich men, and specially such as be sheepmongers, oppress the king's leige people by devouring their common pastures with their sheep ; so that the poor people are not able to keep a cow for the comfort of them and of their poor family, but are like to starve and perish for hunger, if there be not provision made shortly ! What sheepground scapeth these caterpillars of the commonweal ? How swarm they with abundance of flocks of sheep ! and yet when was wool ever so dear, or mutton of so great a price ? . . . these greedy wolves and cumberous comorants will either sell their wool and their sheep at their own price, or else they will sell none. Oh, what a diversity is this in the sale of wools, a stone of wool sometime to be sold at eight groats, and now for eight shillings ! And so likewise of the sheep. God have mercy on us ![2]

He describes indignantly the methods of the enclosers :

If they once creep into a town or village they for the most part never cease, till they have devoured and eaten up the whole town. . . . If there be either farm or sheep-ground, upon the which some honest poor man liveth, both he and his family, out he must. Had it must be, whatsoever it cost, though the poor man and all his should go a begging, it lieth so commodiously for our new-come gentleman. If they buy any tenement, and let it out again to the poor man, O how do they rack it and stretch out the rents thereof, almost from a penny to a pound ! yea, and some of them, buying house and land in a town, suffer the houses to fall down, and turn the ground unto pasture, the poor man not having where to hide his head. . . . Some, buying the lordship of a town, handle the inhabitants thereof on such a sort, that they lose divers of their liberties, being in much worse case than they were afore. Thus the poor people be so wrung of these ungentle gentlemen, that the silly souls are like unto dry haddocks. Some Irishman, beholding them, might well think that they came lately out of St. Patrick's purgatory : they are so withered away, even to the hard bones, for cold and hunger.[3]

This policy, pursued unchecked by the new capitalists, enriched them at the expense of the country, with disastrous effect :

[1] *The Jewel of Joy*, P ii, p. 434.
[2] ibid, P ii, p. 432.
[3] *The Fortress of the Faithful*, P ii, pp. 599-600.

F

... when they have gotten many houses and tenements into their hands, yea, whole townships, they suffer the houses to fall into utter ruin and decay ; so that by this means whole towns are become desolate, and like unto a wilderness, no man dwelling there, except it be the shepherd and his dog. . . . I myself know many towns and villages sore decayed ; so that, whereas in times past there were in some town an hundred households, there remain not now thirty ; in some fifty, there are not now ten ; yea (which is more to be lamented), I know towns so wholly decayed, that there is neither stick nor stone standing, as they use to say.

Where many men had good livings, and maintained hospitality, able at all times to help the king in his wars,[1] and to sustain other charges, able also to help their poor neighbours, and virtuously to bring up their children in godly letters and good sciences, now sheep and conies devour altogether, no man inhabitating the aforesaid places. Those beasts which were created of God for the nourishment of man do now devour man.[2]

Such is the sombre picture which Becon gives of the results of the " revolution of the rich against the poor " which was the accompaniment, though not the consequence, of the Reformation. As he contemplates it he feels constrained, though no lover of monks and " monkery", to praise the ejected religious for the management of their estates and the treatment of their tenants. The new landlords, he says,

... abhor the names of monks, friars, canons, nuns, &c.; but their goods they greedily gripe. And yet, where the cloisters kept hospitality, let out their farms at a reasonable price, nourished schools, brought up youth in good letters, they did none of all these things.[3]

Many hundreds of impoverished peasants would have endorsed this significant admission.[4]

---

[1] The decay of the old yeomanry was partly responsible for the intro- duction of foreign mercenaries to serve under the royal standard.

[2] *The Jewel of Joy*, P ii, p. 434. With the last sentence compare the lines from a contemporary ballad :

> *This sheep he is a wicked wight ;*
> *Man, woman and child he devoureth quite.*

[3] *The Jewel of Joy*, P ii, p. 435.

[4] See also, on the agrarian distress, Pollard, *op. cit.*, pp. 28-32 ; R. H. Tawney, *Religion and the Rise of Capitalism*, pp. 137-150 ; G. Constant, *The Reformation in England*, ii, pp. 102-111, and the authorities quoted.

VI

Somerset at least made an attempt to "redress these intolerable pestilences", but he was obstructed at every turn. and at last the people took matters into their own hands. Becon's own county rose in revolt under Robert Kett in the summer of 1549, a few weeks after an insurrection in the West provoked mainly by dislike of religious innovation had engaged the attention of the government. The Norfolk rebels were concerned only with social and economic grievances, however, and appear to have favoured the Reformation.

Becon deals with both rebellions in the dialogue entitled *The Fortress of the Faithful*. True to his teaching on the divine appointment of the civil magistrates and the obedience due to them, he condemns those for whose sufferings he felt so much, when they presumed to act for themselves. He adduces several instances from the scriptures, proving that insurrection has never profited its promoters and that sedition has always been visited by the stern judgment of God, and adds the comment :

> If they had been as well trained up in learning such godly histories, as they were nouseled in hearing popish masses, and such other trifling trumpery, they had raised up no such tragedies. If there had been but the tenth part of true and learned preachers, that there were of popish priests among them,[1] they had never fallen so such disorder.[2]

But Becon has to tread carefully here, for it had been necessary, as we have seen, to restrict preaching, and finally to prohibit it for a time,[3] and he is anxious to clear the licensed preachers in particular of any responsibility for the insurrections :

> *Theophile* : ... [I have] heard it reported that these new preachers, as they call them, through their undiscreet sermons opened a large window unto dissolution of life, and by this means caused

---

[1] This may have had special reference to the Devon rebels.

[2] P ii, p. 595 ; see also pp. 593-595 for Becon's censures upon civil rebellion.

[3] See above, p. 57 ; also the letter from Ridley to preachers in his diocese, *Works* (PS), pp. 334-335. For the conduct of some preachers, see Fuller, *Church History of Britain*, ii, p. 315, and for their inconveniently zealous behaviour, the doings of Thomas Hancock, in J. G. Nichol's *Narratives* ... , p. 71, of which Dixon has a summary, HCE, ii, pp. 533-534.

the common people to aspire and breach unto carnal liberty, which while they hunted, they forgot both themselves and their duty.

Philemon : I will not excuse all preachers. For some, as I have heard, have taken upon them the office of preaching uncalled, unsent ; and such disordered preachers, for the most part, bring all things to a disorder, yea, to an utter confusion. . . . But as I may speak in the faithful and discreet preachers' behalf, which are lawfully sent of the high powers, and called thereunto by the secret motion of God's Spirit in their hearts, howsoever they be reported, certain I am, they never taught such doctrine as should minister occasion to godly people to shake off the zeal of obedience, or to break any good order or politic law.

Christopher : Yet have I heard some preachers, whom I know to be both prudent and faithful, slandered that they by their preaching have caused these uproars.

Philemon : Ye said well, "slandered". Were they preachers, or rather massmongers, that caused the insurrection in Devonshire?

Christopher : Massmongers and papists, as it is reported.[1]

Philemon : Then are the godly preachers free from giving any occasion of that sedition.

Eusebius : But what of Norfolk ?

Philemon : Even in Norfolk also, or elsewhere, I am sure the very rebels themselves will confess, as I have partly heard and known,[2] that the preachers were not the authors nor provokers of their commotion.[3]

The friends have no difficulty in exculpating the godly preachers, and agree that the blame for the risings must be laid at the door of the " new-come gentleman " and his kind. But Becon has poor comfort to offer to his distressed fellow-countrymen ; his doctrine of the civil power blinds him to the inefficiency and corruption of the Council, and prevents him from seeing what was plain to the simple commons—that the people must redress their own wrongs. He would rather have them continue passive under oppression than commit the sin of sedition, and so incur the danger of eternal damnation. But neighbour *Christopher* is the realist :

[1] There were many priests with the insurgents, but laymen seem to have been the chief instigators of this rising. Becon is obviously concerned to magnify the responsibility of the " massmongers".

[2] We do not know whether Becon was in any way involved in the Norfolk revolt, but he would doubtless have reliable sources of information.

[3] P ii, p. 596. Two licensed preachers, Robert Watson and Matthew Parker (later Archbishop of Canterbury) were allowed by the Norfolk rebels to preach in their camp, and tried to dissuade them from their enterprise ; see Dixon, HCE, iii, p. 83.

. . . ye know the common proverbs : " The belly hath no ears " ; " Hunger is sharper than thorn " ; " Necessity is an hard dart " ; " Need maketh the old wife trot " . . . Ye see the unmercifulness of the rich : what, would ye have the poor people starve and die for hunger ?

[*Philemon* : Rather starve and die for hunger][1] as poor Lazar did, than to trouble a commonweal . . . if they have injuries done unto them, if they cannot otherwise be redressed, let them complain to the magistrates and officers of the commonweal, which are appointed to hear men's causes.

Christopher : If the poor oppressed complain to the justices of the peace or such-like in the country where he dwelleth, that hath the injury done unto him, little redress, as I hear, can be had, one so serveth another's turn, even as the mules scratch one another's back.

Philemon : If there be any such partial officers . . . yet remaineth there another refuge, and that is to complain unto the king's majesty and his most honourable council, which without all doubt will both gladly hear their lamentable complaints, and redress their matters according to justice.[2]

With these hollow assurances the subject is dismissed, and the four neighbours pass on to talk of the need for trust in God's providence during times of adversity.

VII

Of Becon's compositions during Edward's reign several have already been mentioned, including *The Jewel of Joy*, a dissertation on the text : " Rejoice in the Lord alway, and again I say, rejoice", which contains much biographical material, and *The Fortress of the Faithful*, with its descriptions of contemporary social conditions. A third proved the most popular of all his works, and is known to have run into at least nineteen editions before 1632. This is *The Sick Man's Salve*,[3] in which *Philemon* and his friends visit the dying *Epaphroditus*. They convince him that he is experiencing in his sickness the loving visitation of God ; he feels his end at hand ; he makes his will, disposing his property virtuously and not forgetting the universities (as we have seen) and the highways, to the repair of which he

---

[1] Omitted in folio ed., and supplied from ed. of 1550.

[2] P ii, pp. 601-602.

[3] From the mention of Becon's children (P iii, p. 93) it seems that the folio ed. version is a revised one.

leaves forty pounds ; instead of providing for masses for his own soul, he orders the preaching of sermons for the benefit of the souls of others ; he forbids superstitious customs and sumptuous displays at his funeral ; he takes leave of his wife, children and servants, makes a full confession of faith and a final act of penitence, and declares his assurance that he is numbered among those predestinated to everlasting life ; and composing himself to die, passes away as *Philemon* prays from *The Flower of Godly Prayers*. This lengthy tract gives Becon many opportunities of denouncing popery and inculcating true religion, and the result is a compendium of the life and faith of the good protestant, valuable for the whole no less than for the sick, for the living no less than for the dying.

The Sick Man's Salve was popular enough to be mentioned by the dramatists. In Jonson's *Silent Woman*, Lady Haughty says, " And one of them, I know not which, was cured with the Sick Man's Salve. . . ."[1] and in *Eastward Ho*, by Marston, Jonson, and Chapman, Wolf says : ". . . he can tell you almost all the stories of the *Book of Martyrs*, and speak you all the *Sick Man's Salve* without book".[2]   There seems to be no foundation, however, for Ayre's statement that Jonson and the wits of his day ridiculed the titles given by Becon to his works.[3]

To his patron the Primate Becon dedicated *A Treatise of Fasting*, in which he confirms from scripture that

> . . . the rulers have authority given them of God to command their subjects to fast, whensoever any urgent cause is offered ; as in the time of battle, hunger, drought, plague, pestilence, &c.; and that the people are bound by God's commandment to obey the magistrates and their ordinances in all such things . . .[4]

The Council had already exercised its divine authority by a proclamation of 16th January, 1548, enjoining a Lenten fast, not only as a religious discipline, but because it assisted cattle breeding and encouraged the fisheries.[5]   In the same year an Act for the keeping of Lent was passed, designed to secure the same object.[6]

---

[1] Act IV, sc. II ; see *Works* (ed. Gifford, 1875), iii, pp. 427-428 and 522.
[2] Act V, sc. II ; see Marston's *Works*, ed. Bullen, iii, p. 107.
[3] P i, p. xv.
[4] P ii, p. 531.
[5] Strype, *Eccl. Mem.*, II, i, pp. 127-129 ; the proclamation is printed in II, ii, pp. 343 ff. See also Dixon, HCE, ii, p. 490.
[6] See Strype, *Eccl. Mem.*, II, i, p. 211, and Dixon, HCE, ii, pp. 547-548.

The Castle of Comfort is interesting because it shows how Becon's views upon penance were altering now the restraining influence of the Six Articles was removed. There is now no exhortation to go to confession, as there was in *A Potation for Lent,* and he would apparently prefer a precatory form of absolution[1] to that wisely retained in the Office for the Visitation of the Sick.

The Principles of the Christian Religion, dedicated to " the most gentle and godly disposed child, Master Thomas Cecil", is a form of short catechism to which scriptural confirmations and probations are added, and *The Physic of the Soul* and *The Christian Knight,* a dialogue between the Knight and Satan, are devotional compositions of the kind in which he excelled. These complete the works known to have been written by Becon at this time, with the exception of a Latin poem in commendation of William Turner's *Preservative or Triacle against the poison of Pelagius.* Bale attributes two other works to Becon, *Preparationes ad Eucharistiam* and *Olfactorium Spirituale,* but these, if they were his, are no longer extant.[2]

Finally, mention must be made of the royal licence dated 25th March, 1553, which granted to the celebrated printer John Day permission

> . . . for the printing and reprinting of all such works and books devised and compiled by John [Ponet] now Bishop of Winton, or by Tho. Beacon, professor of Divinity ; so that no such book be in any wise repugnant to the holy scriptures, or proceedings in religion, and the laws of the realm.[3]

VIII

Towards the end of September, 1552, while the second Prayer Book was in the press, John Knox, so it is thought, preached before the King and Council a sermon against

---

[1] P ii, p. 568.

[2] I have given Bale's Latin titles from the *Index* ; it is impossible to tell whether the works themselves were in Latin or in English. The *Olfactorium Spirituale* may perhaps be the *Spiritual Nosegay* attributed to Turner by Foxe, v, p. 567 (but not printed in the list of his works in Cooper, *Athenae*), and by Bale wrongly ascribed to Becon.

[3] See Ames, *Typ. Ant.,* iv, pp. 41-42 ; also Strype, *Eccl. Mem.,* II, ii, p. 114.

kneeling at the Communion. The Council thereupon suspended the printing of the Prayer Book, but Cranmer refused to reconsider the rubric which ordered the kneeling, and inveighed against the " glorious and unquiet spirits " who were bent on stirring up trouble. The matter seems to have been discussed again at a Council meeting on 20th October, and at the same meeting the royal chaplains and others were asked to consider and report on the XLV Articles. Some, including Knox, objected to Article XXXVIII *de libro Ceremoniarum Ecclesiae Anglicanae* on the ground that it seemed to express approval, *inter alia*, of the kneeling at the Communion which the new Prayer Book expressly ordered. They therefore composed a Memorial to the Council, in which they asserted their conviction that kneeling at least ought not to be required, being in their judgment inconsistent with scripture. The second part of this Memorial sets forth the reasons " Why the sytting in the action of the Lord's Table is preferred to knelyng". After showing why it is that

> . . . taught by Christ's example at his holie Table, we syt as men placed in quyetnes, and in full possession of our kingdome,

there follows, to quote Dr. Peter Lorimer,

> . . . further argument of a very ingenious and interesting, if not very convincing kind, founded upon the resemblances and differences between the Passover and the Eucharist, and which has all the appearance of having been traced by a different pen from that of Knox—the pen, it seems highly probable, of the excellent Thomas Becon . . .[1]

The Memorial seems to have produced some effect, for on 27th October the Council ordered the insertion in the Prayer Book of a Declaration on Kneeling which retained the practice, but explained that it did not imply

> . . . any adoracion . . . eyther vnto the Sacramentall bread or wyne there bodelye receyued, or vnto anye reall and essenciall presence there beeyng of Chrystes naturall fleshe and bloude.[2]

and Knox felt obliged to explain to his old congregation at Berwick why he had conformed to a Book which did not abolish kneeling outright.

---

[1] *John Knox and the Church of England*, p. 116. The Memorial is printed in full on pp. 267-274.
[2] Brightman, *op. cit.*, ii, p. 721.

Lorimer suggests that Roger Hutchinson may also have shared in the writing of the Memorial, and that he and Becon were both probably acquainted with the ideas on the reception of the Sacrament later included by Laski in his *Brevis et dilucida de Sacramentis Ecclesiae Christi Tractatio* and *Forma ac Ratio tota Ecclesiastici Ministerii* . . ., ideas which would undoubtedly have influenced Knox.[1] So far as Becon is concerned, Lorimer bases his case upon certain resemblances between the Memorial on the one hand, and the *New Catechism* and *The Displaying of the Popish Mass* on the other, which indicate, in his opinion, that Becon was one of the few divines likely at that time to have held views similar to those of Knox, and to have joined with him in advocating them.

There are, however, several objections to Lorimer's theory. In the first place, the similarities between the Memorial and the works mentioned are not sufficient to warrant the inference that *in 1552* Becon's attitude to kneeling at the Communion resembled that of Knox. In the Memorial the significance of the fact that the Passover was eaten standing and the Supper sitting is discussed at some length. At the Passover

> . . . there was one ceremonye notable, that hastilye they should eate the Lambe standyng, theyr loynes gyrded, with staves in their handes ; the Holie Ghost signyfying thereby their sodayne departure from Egypt, the travell and labours they shuld and did susteyne, togyther wythe the defence of God in their journey towards the land of Canaan ; in possession whereof albeit Joshua brought their fathers, yet was not the ceremonye chaunged, but did continewe during the generation, because the veray Joshua that was to leade the elect people of God in[to] all rest and full possession of the kyngdom promissed was not then come in fleshe. But at suche tyme as the Sonne of God began to be preached and revealed to the world . . . began the fygures of the law to evanysshe and to cease.

Circumcision then yielded to baptism, and the Passover to the Lord's Supper, at which Christ

> . . . appereth to have dissolved and disannulled the ceremonye of standing before used at God's commandment in that Sacrament. For . . . the Passover that night was not eatyn standing . . . but sittynge, to witness that [he] who is the end of the lawe to every

[1] The *Brevis* . . . *Tractatio* appeared in 1552 and the *Forma ac Ratio* . . . in 1555. The substance of the former had been preached from the pulpit of Austin Friars before publication ; see Lorimer, *op. cit.*, p. 289.

believer by his travell and dolor was shortly to pass before his
brethren to the kingdom whereunto they should be fully possessed
by Him. For so he manefestly declared : *Desiderio desideravi hoc
Pascha manducare vobiscum antequam patiar* : " most inwardly I
have desyred to eate this Passover with you before I suffer".
It is to be noted that he sayth *this* Passover, as he wold saye, the
ceremonye of other Passovers is here omitted : we sytt as men
possessed in rest, and do not stand as men having a long, desysful
and tedious journay ; menyng that the journay and travell of
the sonnes of God was almost at an end in Himself . . .[1]

So, somewhat abbreviated, runs the argument of the
Memorial. Compare now what Becon writes in *The Displaying
of the Popish Mass* :

. . . the Jews, when they received their sacrament, I mean the
paschal lamb (which was also a figure of Christ to come and to be
slain, as ours is a sign and token that he is already come, slain,
and gone), stood upon their feet with their loins girded and
staves in their hands, to signify not only that they were strangers
and pilgrims in this world, and had here no dwelling-city, but
also that there was a further journey yet to go in the religion of
God, and that other sacraments were to be looked for. But Christ
and his disciples did sit at their supper, to declare that all things
afore figured in the law are now perfectly fulfilled in Christ, that
Lamb of God, which was " slain from the beginning of the
world", and that there are no more sacraments to be looked for,
nor none other doctrine to be enquired for, neither the Jews'
Talmuth, nor Mahomet's Alkaron, nor the pope's Decretals, nor
yet the Emperor's Interim, but that doctrine only which Christ
hath already taught and left in writing by the hands of his
apostles. . . . Therefore doth Christ with his apostles sit at the
receiving of the sacrament, and not stand, after the manner of
the Jews ; even as they, which, travelling by the way, are come
unto their journey's end, are wont to sit down and to take their
rest. Here we have an example of Christ to sit at the Lord's
table, when we receive the holy communion.[2]

In the *New Catechism* exactly the same points are made,
though at greater length.[3]   Between these works and the
Memorial there is obviously a similarity of idea, but no one
would infer from the style and the argument of the latter,
especially when read in its entirety, that anything in it came
from " the pen . . . of the excellent Thomas Becon".

[1] Lorimer, *op. cit.*, pp. 272-273.
[2] P iii, p. 260.
[3] P ii, pp. 298-299.

Of greater weight than literary considerations, moreover, is the absence of evidence that in 1552 Becon had either worked out or adopted any such comparative interpretation of the standing at the Passover and the sitting at the Supper. Lorimer appears to have overlooked the fact that the *New Catechism* was written in 1559 or 1560, and *The Displaying of the Popish Mass* during Becon's exile on the Continent. The latter is reputed to have appeared in a Latin version at Basel in 1559, but it was not published in England prior to its inclusion in the third part of the folio edition in 1563. It is, therefore, less likely that Becon contributed to the Memorial than that he derived his own ideas from it, unless he acquired them from some foreign source during his exile.

Furthermore, Lorimer points out the striking similarity between this part of the Memorial and Laski's *Forma ac Ratio* . . ., which suggests that whoever co-operated with Knox was largely dependent upon certain theories which the Polish reformer had expounded from the pulpit some three years before the publication of his book. It is significant, therefore, that the ideas common to the Memorial and Laski do not all appear in Becon's discussions of the question of kneeling ; for instance, he does not mention the conception of Jesus as the true Joshua.[1]

There is, then, good ground for holding that Becon did not draw up any part of the Memorial. A more difficult question now arises : was he associated in any way with its compilers ? Let us first examine Becon's teaching. There is only one reference to kneeling at the Communion in his Edwardine works, and this tells us nothing ; he does not advocate this or that gesture, but simply shows how the Mass and the Lord's Supper differ :

> Christ delivered the sacrament to his disciples sitting at the table : the papists compel the people to receive it kneeling upon their knees.[2]

During his exile he recalls, without comment, the practice of sitting at the Communion :

[1] Lorimer, *op. cit.*, *cf* pp. 272 and 287.
[2] *The Jewel of Joy*, P ii, p. 455.

O how oft have I seen here[1] in England, at the ministration of
the holy communion, people sitting at the Lord's table after they
have heard the sermon, or the godly exhortation set forth in the
book of common prayer read unto them by the minister . . . [2]

and a few pages later, comparing again the Mass with " Christ
. . . at his supper", he condemns the Papists for deviating from
the Lord's example.[3] Here too there is no indication of Becon's
precise views ; it is simply clear that he prefers sitting to
kneeling :

> . . . although gestures in this behalf seem after some men's
> judgement to be indifferent, yet the nearer we come to Christ's
> order, the better it is : for who can prescribe a more perfect trade
> for all things to be done at and about the ministration of the Lord's
> supper, than that which Christ used himself ?[4]

In another work written on the Continent, *Coenae Sacrosanctae
Domini nostri, et Missae Papisticae, Comparatio*, later translated
into English as *A Comparison between the Lord's Supper and the
Pope's Mass*, Becon merely repeats the points of contrast
already noted in his earlier writings.[5]

The last and fullest expression of Becon's views on this
subject occurs in the *New Catechism*, written some eight years
after the presentation of the Memorial to the Council, where the
matter is discussed in a temperate spirit :

> *Father* : . . . what sayest thou concerning the gestures to be used
> at the Lord's table ?   Shall we receive those holy mysteries
> kneeling, standing, or sitting ?
> *Son* : Albeit I know and confess that gestures of themselves be
> indifferent ; yet I would wish all such gestures to be avoided as
> have outwardly any appearance of evil. . . .   And first of all,
> forasmuch as kneeling hath been long used in the church of
> Christ, through the doctrine of the papists, although of itself it
> be indifferent to be or not to be used, yet would I wish that it
> were taken away by the authority of the higher powers.
> *Father* : Why so ?
> *Son* : For it hath an outward appearance of evil. . . .   I would
> wish with all my heart, that either this kneeling at the receiving

---

[1] When this was written Becon was abroad ; " here " may have been
added in the folio edition, or even " here in England", if the original reference
was to the practice at Strasbourg, Frankfort, or Marburg.

[2] *The Displaying of the Popish Mass*, P iii, p. 256.

[3] ibid, P iii, pp. 260 and 261.

[4] ibid, P iii, p. 260.

[5] P iii, pp. 364 and 365 ; *Comparatio*, pp. 40 and 42.

of the sacrament were taken away, or else that the people were taught that that outward reverence was not given to the sacrament and outward sign, but to Christ, which is represented by that sacrament or sign.[1] . . . Standing, which is used in the most part of the reformed churches in these our days, I can right well allow it, if it be appointed by common order to be used at the receiving of the holy communion. . . .[2] Now, as concerning sitting at the Lord's table, which is also used at this day in certain reformed churches, if it were received by public authority and common consent, and might conveniently be used in our churches, I could allow that gesture best. . . .[3] Notwithstanding, as I said before, gestures are free, so that none occasion of evil be either done or offered. In all things which we call indifferent, this rule of St. Paul is diligently to be obeyed : " Abstain from all evil appearance".[4]

From his writings we would judge Becon to have been a moderate advocate of sitting at the Communion who held the various gestures to be in themselves indifferent, but considered kneeling inexpedient and theologically unsatisfactory. Though they may have undergone alteration from time to time, his views, as finally stated in the *New Catechism*, are moderate and conciliatory in tone. Confirmation of this estimate of his attitude to the gestures is provided by the letter to Calvin dated 5th April, 1555, which Becon and others of the Prayer Book party at Frankfort signed :

> . . . when the magistrates lately gave us permission to adopt the rites of our native country, we freely relinquished all those ceremonies which were regarded by our brethren as offensive and inconvenient. For we gave up . . . kneeling at the holy communion . . . and other things of the like character. And we gave them up, not as being impure and papistical, which certain of our brethren often charged them with being, but whereas they were in their own nature indifferent . . . we notwithstanding chose rather to lay them aside than to offend the minds or alienate the affections of the brethren.[5]

Becon seems to have had no difficulty in giving his assent to this mild statement, which stands in strong contrast to the

[1] The Declaration on Kneeling had been omitted from the 1559 Prayer Book, and it is apparently to this that Becon alludes.
[2] Here follows the explanation of the standing at the Passover, cf. above, p. 72.
[3] Here Becon expounds the significance of sitting at the Supper, cf. above, p. 72.
[4] P ii, pp. 298-299.
[5] *Orig. Let.*, ii, pp. 753-754.

inflexible declaration of the Memorialists that " we cannot admit knelyng", to the support of which they bring every theological, exegetical, and practical argument they can muster.

It seems, therefore, very improbable that Becon made common cause with Knox in pressing for the amendment of the Prayer Book. Would Cranmer's chaplain have opposed the Primate in a matter about which the latter felt so strongly ? Would he have joined those " glorious and unquiet spirits " whom the Archbishop had so straitly censured for disturbing things that were quiet and in good order ? Would the signatory to the Calvin letter have subscribed the Memorial, or the confederate of Knox in London have withstood him in Frankfort ? We can only conclude that Becon had no hand at all in the affair, though he may have been to some extent in sympathy with the promoters of the agitation against kneeling.[1]

Perhaps a suggestion may be permitted in conclusion. Was Becon, as Cranmer's chaplain, one of those who persuaded the Primate to make some concession to the Memorialists ? Such a role would accord better with his known views than that, assigned to him by Dr. Lorimer, of composer of part of the Memorial.   If Becon himself had been partly responsible for the Declaration on Kneeling, it would explain his apparent reference to its omission from the Elizabethan Prayer Book.[2]

[1] In his attempt to father part of the Memorial on Becon, Lorimer seems to have overlooked the similarity between that document and Hooper's interpretation of the sitting at Communion, see Sermon vi on Jonah, *Early Writings* (PS), pp. 536-537. This was composed in 1550 ; Hooper's views became more and more extreme, and he may well have collaborated with Knox.

[2] See above, pp. 74-75.

ÆTATIS
SVÆ · 41
AN°·DNI
· 1553 ·

THOMAS BECONVS SACROSAC
TÆ THEOLOGIÆ PROFESSOR ·

Ora expreſſa vides , viuos imitantia vultus,
Quod potuit calimo, pictor, & arte vides.
Mentis quam nullus potuit tibi reddere pictor,
Effigiem ſcriptis, præbuit ipſe ſuis.

CHAPTER VII

IMPRISONMENT AND EXILE, 1553-1558

I

W HEN Mary came to the throne she assured the Council that in matters of religion she was resolved to use persuasion and not compulsion, hoping by means of zealous and eloquent preachers to win her subjects from their errors.[1] The first to go to the work of conversion was Gilbert Bourn, Archdeacon of London, who preached at Paul's Cross on 13th August what Foxe calls " a seditious sermon . . . to set popery abroad".[2] This discourse was not at all to the liking of the audience, and a tumult ensued during which Bourn was menaced, and appealed to John Bradford to speak to the people and quiet them. Taking Bourn's place, Bradford managed to secure order, and afterwards saw that the preacher was conducted to safety.[3] The mob then dispersed peaceably and, assembling again in the afternoon at Bow church to hear Bradford, was severely reproved for its riotous conduct that morning.[4]

On the Wednesday following, 16th August, Bradford was committed to the Tower,[5] and the same day he was joined by Veron and Becon, both designated " seditious preachers".[6] The latter's offence is not stated, but he may have been in some

[1] See Foxe, vi, p. 392, and cf Mary's first proclamation on 18th August, in Gee and Hardy, *Documents*, p. 374.

[2] vii, p. 144.

[3] For accounts of this affair, see Machyn's *Diary*, p. 41 ; Foxe, vi, pp. 391-392, and vii, p. 144 ; Bradford's own story, *Works* (PS), i, p. 485 ; Strype, *Eccl. Mem.*, III, i, pp. 32-33 ; Haweis, *Sketches of the Reformation*, pp. 35-36.

[4] See Bradford, *Works* (PS), i, pp. 485-486 ; Foxe, vii, p. 145.

[5] For the charges against him, see his first examination before Gardiner, *Works* (PS), i, p. 465.

[6] Foxe, vi, pp. 538 and 756 ; Strype, *Eccl Mem.*, III, i, p. 77 ; *Cranmer*, p. 397.

way involved in the disturbance of the previous Sunday. In any case, it was doubtless considered expedient to silence him as soon as possible ; it would have been inconvenient for a preacher and writer of his power and popularity to remain at large at so critical a time, and his earlier record would mark him as a man to be watched. In the Tower, Becon and his companions found Ridley, Sandys and Cox, and from time to time they were joined by others, notably Latimer and Cranmer.[1]

Meanwhile the work of annulling the Reformation went forward, and amongst other measures proceedings were taken against the married clergy, who now comprised, it has been supposed, about one-fifth of the total number. On 15th March, 1553-4, in pursuance of the Queen's Injunctions, sentences of suspension, sequestration, and deprivation were pronounced at Canterbury against the Archdeacon, three prebendaries, two preachers, and two minor canons, and all were forbidden to cohabit with their wives. Three other prebendaries and the four remaining preachers, among them Thomas Becon, did not appear, and were declared contumacious. Some could not appear, being in prison, and others had fled, but all were deprived.[2] At the same time Becon must have been ejected from his Rectory of St. Stephen, Walbrook, for a new appointment to the living was made on 2nd May, 1554.[3] The proceedings at Canterbury are the first intimation that Becon had taken to himself a wife, though we know nothing of the details of his marriage.[4]

Becon's imprisonment, which he describes as " long and . . . most miserable", and attended by

> . . . other afflictions wherewith I was daily accumbered, besides the deceitful assaults of Satan and of his ministers, wherewith I was without ceasing troubled and disquieted, not only outwardly, but also inwardly . . .[5]

came to an end on 22nd March, 1553-4.[6] His release cannot

[1] See Knox's *A godly letter sent too the fayethfull in London, &c., Works*, iii, pp. 187-188 ; he spells Becon's name, *Bacon*.

[2] Strype, *Cranmer*, pp. 471-472.

[3] Newcourt, *Repertorium*, i, p. 540 : " Will. Ventris, 2nd May 1554, per priv. Bekon."

[4] Becon's marriage is more fully discussed in chapter xi.

[5] Preface, *A Comfortable Epistle* . . ., P iii, p. 204.

[6] The date of Becon's release is often, for some reason, given wrongly as 24th March.

have been widely known, for early in April Ridley, who had
been moved to the Bocardo in Oxford, asks Bradford about the
Tower prisoners :

> We long to hear of father Crome, Doctor Sandys, Master
> Saunders, Veron, Becon, Rogers, &c.[1]

Regarding Becon's liberation, which he celebrated by a versification of Psalm 103,[2] there is no less mystery than about
certain other passages in his life. Foxe, our sole informant,
says :

> . . . how hardly escaped he with his life out of the Tower, had not
> God's providence blinded Winchester's eyes, in mistaking his
> name ![3]

What this means, it is impossible even to guess. Gardiner may
have released him in error, but this is unlikely. If, however,
Becon had not committed any grave misdemeanour, but was
simply under precautionary arrest, Gardiner, following his
usual method,[4] may have judged it expedient to give him an
opportunity of leaving the country. So " after . . . skulking
about for some time, at length he saved himself by exile",[5]
and made his way to Strasbourg.[6]

II

A very important group of exiles eventually came together
in Strasbourg : Sir John Cheke, Sir Peter Carew, Sir Thomas
Wrothe, Sir Anthony Cooke, Sir Richard Morison, Dr. Sandys,
Thomas Sampson, John Ponet, and the bankers Thomas Heton
and John Abell, among others.[7]   Peter Martyr and Pierre
Alexandre had arrived in the autumn of 1553, and in the spring
of the next year they were joined by a number of students
and other refugees. How soon Becon reached the city we do
not know, but he made a notable addition to the colony which
seems to have been planned by Cecil as a centre for political

---

[1] Bradford, *Works* (PS), ii, p. 83.
[2] A versification of Ps. 112 may also belong to this time.
[3] v, p. 696.
[4] See Garrett, *Exiles*, pp. 11-12.
[5] Strype, *Cranmer*, i, p. 608. Strype gives no authority for his statement.
[6] In company with Ponet ? See Garrett, *Exiles*, p. 84.
[7] ibid, pp. 27-28, and also the biographies in the Census.

G

propaganda.[1] It cannot have been merely chance or con-
venience that led him to Strasbourg ; his value as an experienced
and serviceable propagandist suggests that after his liberation
he was directed to make his way thither and to place his talents
at the disposal of the cause.

The Argentian divines were not long idle, and before many
weeks had passed the products of their summer's labour were
being conveyed into England by way of Emden, augmented
there by Bale's scurrilous and obscene *Declaration of Edmonde
Bonners Articles.* The arrival of these seditious exports seems
to have been timed with the object of arming opinion against
the anticipated reconciliation with the Roman see, and of
influencing the deliberations of the Parliament then due to meet.
Among these books was a pamphlet, *The humble and unfained
confession of the belefe of certain poore banished men,* which was
written by Ponet, though Becon, Sandys, and Sampson may
have collaborated in its production.[2]

The tracts which found so ready a sale in London no doubt
included two from Becon's pen, *A comfortable epistle to the
afflicted people of God,* and *An humble supplication unto God for
the restoring of his holy word unto the Church of England.*[3] The
first, to which the author added a preface in 1563,[4] was, as he
assures us, " not read of the brethren without fruit". It is in
a familiar strain, ascribing the present distress and persecution
to England's unthankfulness for God's past mercies ; enjoining
repentance, faith, good works, prayer, and patience ; and
fortifying the reader with many scriptural instances proving
that in the time of extremity God will act, if man will but
return to him.

But the *Supplication* strikes a new note, and one sounded
with unwelcome frequency during Becon's latter years. He
explains that in his writing after 1554

---

[1] Garrett, *Exiles,* pp. 27-29.

[2] See ibid, pp. 28-29, 84, 142, and 254-255.

[3] Dixon seems to have thought that possibly these works, and certainly
others, like *The Displaying of the Popish Mass,* were written prior to Becon's
flight to the Continent, but internal evidence alone tells against this view ;
see HCE, iv, p. 684.   C. H. Smyth, *Cranmer and the Reformation under
Edward VI,* p. 7, confuses Becon's *Humble Supplication* with the anonymous
Supplicacyon to the Quenes maiesty, which he erroneously attributes to him.

[4] " From Cantorbury, October 6", P iii, p. 204.

. . . as the time and manners of men justly required, I have somewhat more sharped my pen in some places against antichrist and his Babylonical brood, than in my books heretofore made and published.[1]

It might better have been said that he had tasted of that polluted fount of inspiration from which Bale, Ponet, and their kind took such copious draughts, and had accommodated his style to that of some of the men in whose company he found himself. The *Supplication*, in fact, is less a prayer than a presumptious and blasphemous harangue addressed to the Almighty :

Thou callest thyself a " jealous God " : why then dost thou suffer thy people . . . to be thus seduced and led away from thee . . . ? Thou callest thyself a Lord, and thou sayest that thou wilt give thy glory to none other, nor thy praise unto graven images : how cometh it then to pass that thou sufferest thy glory so to decay in the realm of England . . . ? Thou callest thyself a lion and " a consuming fire", and threatenest utter destruction unto thine adversaries : why sufferest thou then these antichrists thus to rise, roar, and rage against the testament of thy most dear Son . . . ?[2]

This passage alone shows the offensive spirit which animates the *Supplication*, and many other choice specimens of the pious author's devotional style could be given. He describes, with coarse and unseemly comment, every detail of the old services, now restored to use again[3] ; he complains of the treatment of the married clergy, and denounces as " filthy dogs " those who have put away their wives[4] ; he compares Mary with Jezebel, the faithful ministers and godly preachers with the prophets of the Lord, and the Romish priests with the priests of Baal ;[5] but he reserves his best abuse for " a certain head wolf clothed in a bishop's rotch " who can be none other than Gardiner, and I cannot forbear quoting part of this. Winchester is portrayed as

. . . that great wolf, whose face is like unto the face of a she-bear that is robbed of her young ones, whose eyes continually burn with the unquenchable flames of the deadly cockatrice, whose

---

[1] Preface to the folio edition, P i, p. 29.
[2] P iii, p. 226.
[3] See, for example, his account of baptism, P iii, p. 231.
[4] P iii, p. 235.
[5] P iii, p. 238, *cf* p. 239.

teeth are like to the venomous toshes of the ramping lion, whose mouth is full of cursed speaking and bitterness, whose tongue speaketh extreme blasphemies against thee and thy holy Anointed, whose lips are full of deadly poison, whose throat is an open sepulchre, whose breath foameth and bloweth out threatening and slaughter against the disciples of the Lord, whose heart without ceasing imagineth wickedness, whose hands have a delight to be imbrued with the blood of the saints, whose feet are swift to shed blood, whose whole man, both body and soul, go always up and down musing of mischief. This wolf, O Lord, is so arrogant, haughty, and proud, seeing the government of the whole realm is committed unto him, that he hath cast away all fear of thee. . . . When such, O Lord, as will not obey their popish and devilish proceedings, are brought before that grievous wolf, they are miserably taunted, mocked, scorned, blasphemed, as thy dearly-beloved Son was in bishop Caiphas' house, and afterward cruelly committed to prison, to the Tower, to the Fleet, to the Marshalseas, to the King's Bench, to the Counters, to Lollards' Tower, to Newgate, &c., where they are kept as sheep in a pinfold appointed to be slain. And as this cruel and bloody wolf dealeth with the poor lambs, even so do the residue of that lecherous litter.[1]

If it wants something of the colour and force (not to mention the blasphemy and obscenity) of Bale's best efforts, the reader will at least allow that the *Supplication* is not altogether an unworthy imitation of the pungent and scurrilous invective of which his lordship of Ossory was a master.

As a prayer, of course, the *Supplication* is outrageous, and as an account of the state of affairs in England it is biased and exaggerated. But we miss the whole point of the work when we pause to criticize its devotional propriety or its historical accuracy. It was designed simply to stir up anti-Romanist feeling in England, and to excite and encourage the resistance of those who remained there. And we may be sure that Becon had an eye upon Continental opinion. The enormities which he describes in such vivid language would support the legend of persecution and banishment for religion which the exiles had put about,[2] and would help to allay any suspicions which the German civic authorities were inclined to entertain concerning the political character of the migration from England.

[1] P iii, p. 237, *cf* p. 228.
[2] See Garrett, *Exiles*, p. 15.

It is important as an example of the sort of interpretation the refugees were placing upon events, and of the propaganda by which they hoped to influence the course of affairs at home.

This is well illustrated by Becon's attitude to Queen Mary, and to the " monstruous regiment of women". He was not the only one to set John Knox's trumpet to his lips, for Ponet[1] and Christopher Goodman,[2] his companions in exile at Strasbourg, blew a note even stronger and more sustained, while Bartholomew Traheron[3] from Frankfort gave no uncertain sound.[4] Of their arguments, Becon stresses only one : that Mary was a woman, and born therefore not to rule but to be in subjection to men ; but he does not disguise the implications of his thesis. Though women sometimes ruled over God's people, yet such queens were

> . . . for the most part wicked, ungodly, superstitious, and given to idolatry and to all filthy abominations ; as we may see in the histories of queen Jesabel, queen Athalia, queen Herodias, and such like.[5]

The twenty-two comparisons between the times of Mary and of Jezebel which occupy almost half the *Supplication* insinuate that as the lives and acts of those queens agree, so also must their ends.

Becon is silent upon a subject to which Goodman and Ponet address themselves at length, that of the ultimate sovereignty of the people and their right to resume power which they have delegated to unfit rulers.[6] But in the *Comfortable Epistle* he encourages a practice apparently common in the secret assemblies which continued to meet in England and to use the Prayer Book—prayer, either for the queen's conversion from idolatry, or for her speedy decease.[7] Recounting from the book of Esther how Ahasuerus had been turned from his purpose of persecuting the Jews, and had given them leave to execute vengeance upon any who troubled them, he adds a marginal

---

[1] *A shorte Treatise of politike pouuer.* . . .
[2] *How superior powers oght to be obeyd of their subiects.* . . .
[3] *A Warning to England to repente.* . . .
[4] On this aspect of Puritan politics, see Maitland, *op. cit.*, pp. 126-149.
[5] P iii, see pp. 227-228
[6] See Maitland, *op. cit.*, Essay VI, and esp. pp. 111-112.
[7] See Dixon, HCE, iv, pp. 287 and 298-299 ; 1 *Phil. and Mary* 9 enacted against these schismatical meetings and their practices.

note which is certainly a veiled incitement to pray for Mary's repentance or death :

> May not God thus work in the queen's heart for his faithful servants in time to come ? or else, taking her away, set up such one to reign as may favour his people ?[1]

Generally, however, he seems to have left to the more competent pens of his fellow exiles the production of the political propaganda which began to flood into England in the autumn of 1554.

III

Meanwhile, other refugees had settled in Frankfort and, under the leadership of William Whittingham, decided to adopt a Calvinistic form of worship and church polity. They then invited the exiles in Strasbourg, Zurich, Duisburg, and Emden to come and share the godly order they proposed to establish, and at the same time elected three ministers to undertake the oversight of the congregation, Knox, now at Geneva, being one. These proceedings were regarded with some apprehension by the supporters of episcopacy and the second Edwardine Prayer Book, and Strasbourg and Zurich began to take steps to counteract the developments in Frankfort. Letters and envoys passed between the colonies without gaining any advantage for either party, and the first stage of the " troubles " ended with the breaking off of negotiations by Strasbourg, and the setting up in Frankfort of a " right reformed church " under the ministry of Knox.[2]

Neither of the letters written from Strasbourg to Frankfort (23rd November and 13th December, 1554) bears Becon's name among the signatures, nor does it appear in the list of English refugees furnished by the city magistrates on 28th December to the Duke of Württemberg.[3] Another notable omission from the correspondence, the list of refugees, and the Strasbourg protocols is the name of Richard Cox, a man of

---

[1] P iii, p. 214.
[2] For full accounts of the affairs at Frankfort, see *Troubles* ; also an edition by E. Arber, 1908, with notes and many additions ; also Dixon, HCE, iv, pp. 688-699, J. H. Colligan, *William Whittingham* . . ., and Garrett, *Exiles*.
[3] Garrett, *Exiles*, p. 85.

wide liturgiological experience, who had arrived in Strasbourg in June, 1554, or thereabout.[1] What took Becon and Cox away from the city that winter ?—for it is unlikely that the former, at any rate, would have left before the end of September, being occupied with Ponet and others in the production of subversive pamphlets.

It seems probable that Cox had been despatched on diplomatic missions supplementary to those of Richard Chambers and Edmund Grindal, who visited Frankfort in November. His task, for which he was eminently fitted, may have been to keep the other colonies, and particularly Zurich, informed of the way the situation developed, and to plan action in the event of the negotiations breaking down. Everything points to the existence of a carefully organized campaign directed from Strasbourg, perhaps by Ponet himself, at the details of which we can now only guess. Some hint of Cox's work behind the scenes may be seen in the fact that he had not long been in Frankfort before he summoned Horne from Zurich to his assistance ;[2] the future Bishop of Winchester may well have been waiting in readiness for this call.

The position which he later occupied at Frankfort, and his well-known experience and ability in " underground " work, suggests that Becon may have been associated with Cox on at least some of his journeys. In the intervals, having no propaganda to prepare, he may have taken the opportunity to visit his wife and family, who by this time were no doubt established in Marburg.[3]

Negotiations having proved futile, Strasbourg determined upon direct and forceful intervention. On 13th March, 1554-5, Dr. Cox, arrogant and domineering, arrived in Frankfort with a party which probably included Thomas Becon. Immediately they proceeded to reduce the church to order. They began to answer aloud after the minister, declaring that

... they woulde do as they had donne in Englande, and that they woulde haue the face off an English churche.[4]

[1] Garrett, *Exiles*, p. 134.
[2] ibid, p. 189.
[3] See below, p. 91.
[4] *Troubles.* p. xxxviii.

and on the following Sunday one of their number ascended the pulpit and read the Litany, the Coxians making the responses. Knox was not slow to meet the challenge ; it was his turn to preach that afternoon, and having in his exposition of Genesis appropriately come to " Noah as he laie open in his tente", he delivered an outspoken sermon to the effect that

> . . . as diuers thinges . . . ought to be kepte secret, euenso suche thinges as end to the dishonor off God and disquieting of his churche ought to be disclosed and openly reproued.

He then denounced the visitors from Strasbourg for their interference, and they, as he came down from the pulpit, " verye sharplie charged, and reproued " him. Conferences and disputations followed, but broke up when Cox insisted on the retention of the versicles and responses at the beginning of Mattins, and Knox lost his temper.[1]

The congregation then submitted the matter to the arbitration of the Frankfort magistrates in a Latin *Supplication*, the conclusion of which is significant :

> But wherfore speake yow off theis thinges will yow saie, that apperteneth nothinge to vs ? yes verely, we thinke it touchethe yow verie moche, for yff thies men armed by your authoritie shall do what they liste, this euill shalbe in time established by yow and neuer be redressed, nether shall there for euer be anie ende of this controuersie in Englande. But yff it woulde please your honorable authoritie to decree this moderation between vs . . . not we alone . . . but oure whole posteritie, yea oure whole englishe nation, and all good men, to the perpetuall memorie off your names, shalbe bownde vnto yow for this great benefit.[2]

Neither party, it is clear, regarded the controversy simply as a local wrangle over the worship of the English church in Frankfort. They knew that when the tyranny was overpast they would return home to continue their interrupted work, and were well aware that upon the issue of the present contest would depend the character of the Church of England of the future. Nor did events prove them wrong, for the troubles begun at Frankfort were not brought to an end until more than a century had elapsed.

---

[1] Cox declared, " Ego volo habere " ; afterwards Knox said, " Who was most blameworthy, God shall judge ; and if I spake fervently, to God was I fervent " ; *Works*, iv, p. 46.

[2] *Troubles*, pp. XLII-XLIII.

The magistrates reminded the exiles of the conditions upon which they had been granted the privilege of residence, and ordered them to conform to the doctrine and ceremonies of the French church, on pain of expulsion from the city. To this, Cox agreed, with the object of gaining time.[1] He then entered upon the final stage of his campaign. Certain treasonable passages in Knox's works were brought to the attention of the magistrates, and he was advised to leave Frankfort—otherwise, they said, they would have no alternative but to hand him over to the Emperor. Thus threatened, Knox did not delay his going, but left the city on 26th March, 1555. The magistrates then sanctioned the use of the Prayer Book, and the triumphant Cox told the clergy who assembled on 28th March to elect officers for the church that

> . . . for the order, it was already determined, and other order then the booke off Englande they shulde not haue. . . .[2]

Becon does not figure in these proceedings by name, but there can be no doubt that he was active in support of Cox. He signed the letter written to Calvin on 5th April, wherein the Prayer Book party gave their version of the events of the preceding month, suspecting that a prejudiced version might have reached Geneva,[3] and also (as " Minister of the Word of God ") a second letter, despatched on 20th September.[4] From the latter it would seem that he had been appointed one of the two Ministers to whom, with a Pastor, four elders, and two deacons, the government of the church had been entrusted by the meeting of 28th March already mentioned.

Reference has been made to the first of these two letters to Calvin,[5] and the second is no less firm in its attitude to ceremonial matters :

> . . . these [English ceremonies], indeed, we pertinaciously retain, as knowing them to be very godly : this, however, has never been done by us in a precise manner ; for we have abandoned some of them for the sake of your friends. . . .[6]

[1] Colligan, *op. cit.*, p. 55, describes Cox's action as " inexplicable", but his motive was clearly to avoid at all costs being sent back to Strasbourg.
[2] *Troubles*, p. XLVII.
[3] *Orig. Let.*, ii, p. 755.
[4] ibid, p. 763.
[5] See above, p. 75.
[6] *Orig. Let.*, ii, pp. 756-757.

Our ceremonies are very few, and all of them of no little use towards the advancement of godliness. . . .[1]

That Becon could subscribe these letters shows that he had thrown in his lot with the moderate party of the English Reformation, and upheld the order of 1552. His position as Minister or Preacher in the church at Frankfort, moreover, is evidence that he was regarded as a firm supporter of the policy sponsored by the exiles of Strasbourg and by many also from Zurich, while as a former chaplain of Archbishop Cranmer he must have possessed considerable prestige in the eyes of those who stood for the maintenance of the Primate's principles and the furtherance of his work.

In view of this, it is surprising that Becon is not once mentioned in the narrative of the *Troubles*, and that we have no record of his ministry in Frankfort, especially when other names less eminent occur again and again. The omission may simply be due to coincidence, but an alternative explanation should not be overlooked—that, when the account of the troubles came to be written, twenty years after, Becon's name was suppressed. He had already shown a preference for sitting at the reception of the Sacrament, and subsequently, in the *New Catechism*, he made it clear that he regarded kneeling as a gesture unsuited to the times. In Elizabeth's reign, at a memorable session of Convocation, he joined with others in demanding the abolition of certain ceremonies and usages, and the adoption of various disciplinary measures, and after that, was involved in the troubles over vestments. His attitude to these questions and the character of much of his writing no doubt disposed the Puritans to regard him as one who had advocated their principles, and by historians and biographers he has generally been classed as a Puritan, due, it seems to me, to a misunderstanding of his real position. It is not unlikely that when the events at Frankfort came to be related the author, desirous of claiming Becon as a supporter of the Puritan cause, felt it undesirable that he should be shown as a fervent adherent of Cox's party. The easiest course was therefore adopted, and he was not mentioned at all.

[1] *Orig. Let.*, ii, p. 758.

IV

Becon remained in Frankfort for some time after the Coxian victory, and is said to have lived in the Horsemarket.[1] Presumably he continued his work of preaching and writing, and despatches from England would have brought him news that a royal proclamation of 13th June, 1555, against heretical books had again named him among the authors prohibited.[2] When and why he left Frankfort we do not know. He may have accompanied some of the " lerned men " who had been in conference there about the revision of the liturgy, or he may have gone with Cox to Zurich at the end of November. During the winter of 1555 or early in the following spring he may have determined to settle in Marburg, his connexion with which lasted, he says, almost three years.

He was certainly in Strasbourg for a time during the summer of 1556. A royal commission was issued on 16th June of that year for the delivery of " certeyne letters and commaundmentes under their Maiestyes pryvy seale " to eleven of the exiles, and one John Brett was entrusted with its execution. Journeying over Europe with little success, Brett arrived at Strasbourg on 30th August. There, he says,

> . . . oute of the same house[3] I met with one callid Becon excepte
> I be greatly disceaved. He amongest other thinges had tolde me
> I mighte perhapps repent myne enterprise, and that he wolde not
> haue bene in my cote for a thowsand poundes to haue commed to
> deliver any letteres in those parties.[4]

The rest of Becon's exile was spent in Marburg,[5] where he enjoyed the patronage of Philip, Landgrave of Hesse, and his

---

[1] Garrett, *Exiles*, pp. 54 and 85.

[2] Foxe, vii, p. 127 ; Strype, *Eccl. Mem.*, III, i, p. 418. The proclamation had " Theodore Basil, otherwise called Thomas Beacon " ; is this simply a precautionary prohibition, copied from the proclamation of 1546, or was literature appearing in Mary's reign which bore the name of Basil ? The prohibition would be more likely to apply to Becon's recent works than to those written under Henry VIII.

[3] Richard Cooke's ; see Garrett, *Exiles*, p. 126.

[4] Brett's *Narrative of the pursuit of English refugees in Germany under Q. Mary* ; see Leadam, in *Transactions of the R. Hist. Soc.*, new series, xi (1897), p. 131.

[5] *Bale, Catalogus*, p. 757. Becon seems to have been the only English exile resident at Marburg.

son William.   Dedicating to the latter the treatise *Coenae sacrosanctae Domini Jesu Christi, et Missae Papisticae, Comparatio,* he gives as one of his reasons for so doing,

> . . . quod hic in Academia tua politioribus litteris ut florentissima, ita viris insigniter doctis haud parum referta, triennium fere cum familia agens, constanti fama atque omnium sermone celebratum acceperim. . . .

It seems that Becon returned for the last period of his exile to the tutorial work in which he had already spent so much time, and no doubt most of the Latin compositions listed by Bale in his *Catalogus* were written at Marburg.[1]

The passage just quoted has two points of interest.   The preface to the *Comparatio* is dated " Marpurgi, ex Museo nostro, mense Februarii Anno Christi 1559",[2] and the colophon shows that it was printed in 1559[2] by Oporinus of Basel.   Becon was still in Marburg, therefore, three months after Elizabeth's accession, and did not finally return to England until March or April, 1559.   This, by his somewhat rough methods of computation, more or less accounts for the *triennium* he mentions.   He must have taken up residence in Marburg in the spring of 1556, and his presence in Strasbourg in the August of that year was due, no doubt, to a passing visit.   Since his son Basil was baptized in St. Stephen's, Walbrook, on 14th January, 1558-9, it is possible that Becon paid a brief visit to England in December, 1558, and returned to the Continent immediately after the baptism.

What of Becon's family during these years ?   If his wife and children escaped with him, they did not go to Strasbourg or Frankfort, for no mention of them occurs in the records of those cities.   It is difficult to discover what happened in such cases ; Coverdale, for instance, was accompanied by his wife,[3] but Mrs. Sandys came to her husband after he had been one year in exile.[4]   No doubt the procedure varied according to circumstances, and depended in large measure upon the haste with which it was necessary to leave England.   Becon, as we have seen, does not appear to have departed immediately after

---

[1] p. 757 ; see Bib. I, A 41 and A 44-52.
[2] New style.
[3] Garrett, *Exiles*, p. 132.
[4] Foxe, viii, p. 598.

his release from prison, and while " skulking about " may have been making arrangements to take his family with him to Germany. It is not clear what he means by " triennium fere cum familia agens " ; in its context it could refer to his period of residence in the *familia* of learned men and students at Marburg University, but more probably it should be taken in its natural sense, to denote that he lived in Marburg with his family for almost three years.

We may suppose, then, that Becon's wife and at least one small boy, Christophile,[1] either travelled with him or followed at no great interval, and were lodged in Marburg, while Becon himself took up his abode first in Strasbourg and then in Frankfort. In 1556 he secured tutorial work at Marburg University and rejoined his family, whom he had visited from time to time. Christophile, and possibly an elder boy, Theodore, died in exile, but another son, also named Theodore, was born in 1555, and perhaps a daughter, Rachel, before 1558. Towards the end of November in that year, danger then being past, Becon's wife set off for England ; she was shortly expecting delivery of another child, and was probably accompanied by her husband. The six-weeks journey was completed by the beginning of January, and the baby Basil, born either on the way or just after their arrival, was baptized on 14th January, 1558-9.[2] If Becon had crossed to England, he then returned to Marburg and, having settled his affairs there, rejoined his family in the following March or April, and soon settled in Canterbury.

[1] See below, pp. 125-126.
[2] *Register* of St. Stephen's, Walbrook, Harl. xlii, p. 1.

CHAPTER VIII

CANON OF CANTERBURY, 1559-1567

I

WITH the accession of Elizabeth the exiles looked to receive some recognition of their trials and their constancy in support of true religion. Rough lists[1] drawn up by Cecil showed bishoprics, deaneries, canonries, and benefices vacant, and clergy at that time without promotion, and among the latter appears Becon's name, a † indicating that he was one of those marked out for special preferment. But when appointments came to be made, he was passed over. It may be that he had, as Strype says, chosen " to serve God and his church in some privater capacity " ;[2] or it may be that he had begun to abandon the position which he had taken up at Frankfort, and had become suspected of a tendency to nonconformity.[3] But another explanation is possible : he was one of those who had denounced the " monstruous regiment of women", and this probably caused him to be regarded in high quarters with some suspicion as a divine capable of seditious tendencies. The rest, it is true, had silently concurred in the views which Becon and others had expressed, but they had not deliberately put them forward, and they hastened to disown them when Elizabeth came to power.[4] It may well have been for this reason that Becon was not given the preferment that he deserved. Yet he did not go entirely unrewarded, for a prebend fell to him, and some time during 1559 he was collated to the fourth stall in Canterbury Cathedral[5]—probably the

[1] Strype, *Annals*, I, i, pp. 227-229.
[2] ibid, p. 229.
[3] Colligan, *op. cit.*, p. 97.
[4] For an account of Aylmer's attempt to apologize and to extricate the exiles from the predicament into which Elizabeth's accession threw them, see Maitland, *op. cit.*, Essay X.
[5] Le Neve, *Fasti*, i, p. 50 : " Thomas Bacon or Beacon ".

prebend which Cecil had marked as vacant. In possession of
this Becon remained until his death, adding thereto from time
to time certain benefices to which he was presented.

On 21st October, 1560, Becon became Rector of Buckland
in Hertfordshire, but he does not appear to have held the
living long.[1] A more important preferment came his way six
months later, when on 3rd March, 1560-1 he was made Vicar
of Christ Church, Newgate, which he held until his death.[2]
This church, destroyed in the Great Fire of 1666, was reputed
to be one of the most splendid in London, three hundred feet
long, with columns and pavement of marble, and was renowned
for the number of celebrated people buried there.[3] On 3rd[4] or
4th[5] April, 1562, he was admitted to the vicarage of Sturry, a
small village some three miles north-east of Canterbury,[6] and
in the following year he was reinstated in his old living of
St. Stephen's, Walbrook, which he resigned within a little
while.[7] He was then presented to the rectory of St. Dionis
Backchurch by the Dean and Chapter of Canterbury,[8] and
retained this benefice also until his death.[9] This church was
one of the thirteen " peculiars " in the Archdeaconry of London
which belonged to the Archbishop of Canterbury and were
exempt from the jurisdiction of the Bishop and the Archdeacon
of London.

It is curious to find in the ranks of the pluralists and non-
residers one who so constantly inveighed against the evils of

[1] Newcourt, *Repertorium*, i, p. 815 : Thomas Becon on the death of John
Tilney ; then Esdras Bland is shown as Rector, and then, 27th June, 1567,
Edwd. Hicks " per mort Bland".

[2] Newcourt, *Repertorium*, i, p. 318 : Tho. Beaton (*sic*) alias Basell . . .
Hennessy, *Nov. Repert.*, p. 125 : Thomas Beacon or Bekon or Basill, A.B. . . .
then, 28th January, 1567-8, Hy. Bedell (Newcourt—" per mort Beaton ").

[3] There is a fine picture of the church and its surroundings *circ.* 1547 in
the front of the Register transcript, Harl. xxi.

[4] Parker's *Register*, p. 787.

[5] ibid, p. 404.

[6] Becon is listed as not yet having compounded for the firstfruits of this
benefice, ibid, p. 427 (? early in 1564).

[7] Hennessy, *Nov. Repert.*, p. 386 ; Philip Pettit was appointed in Becon's
place on 1st July, 1563.

[8] 10th August, 1563, Strype, *Parker*, i, p. 258 ; Parker's *Register*, p. 434 ;
also p. 802 ; Newcourt, *Repertorium*, i, p. 330 (" per mort Armerar [John
Armeras] ") ; Hennessy, *Nov. Repert.*, p. 125.

[9] Newcourt, *Repertorium,* " Theodore Newton, A.M., 26th Sept., 1567,
per mor. Beacon " ; also Hennessy, *Nov., Repert.*

pluralism and non-residence !¹ The preface to the folio edition
of Becon's works, however, may explain this apparent declen-
sion from principle :

> Pastors were then² resident upon their benefices. . . . Neither
> were they then troubled with many benefices (as the manner
> now-a-days is), but they were content with one ; which one in
> those days was sufficient both for them and for their family, and
> also for the convenient relief of the poor, being far unlike our
> three-half-penny benefices, whereof seven or eight being put
> together will scarcely furnish the pastor with such convenient
> expenses for him, his family, and the poor, as one benefice did in
> those days ; so greatly hath blind superstition and foolish
> devotion increased the number of parish-churches.³

For Becon, who never ceased to bemoan his poverty, this was
doubtless a sufficient cause for adding benefice to benefice.

He soon resumed his activities as a preacher, and Machyn
records in his *Diary* three occasions on which he made the
sermon.⁴ He also preached before the Lord Mayor and Alder-
men in St. Mary Spital without Bishopsgate on 15th April, 1560,⁵
while on 3rd April, 1566, Archbishop Parker wrote to Cecil
regarding the preachers for Holy Week that year :

> . . . for the third day⁶ my lord mayor sent to me praying me to
> obtain of Mr. Beacon (who they hear shall preach at the cross
> this next Sunday⁷) to supply that day. I promised that I would
> move him to satisfy their desire. . . .⁸

These few notices afford only a slight indication of the demand
which must have been made upon his services ; others,
unfortunately, I have not been able to trace.

The first important ecclesiastical duty which fell to Becon
was that of acting as one of the clerical visitors for the south-

---

¹ See *The Jewel of Joy*, P ii, pp. 431-432 ; the preface to *The Fortress of
the Faithful*, P ii, p. 587 ; *The Acts of Christ and of Antichrist*, " Of their
doctrine", P iii, pp. 534-536 ; &c.

² In primitive times.

³ P i, p. 21.

⁴ On 21st October, 1559, at the funeral of the Countess of Rutland (p. 216
and Ellis's *Shoreditch*, p. 75) ; on 16th April, 1560, at the funeral of John Bedy
(p. 231) ; on 20th July, 1562, at a wedding (p. 288); see ed. cit.

⁵ Cooper, *Athenae*, i, p. 247.

⁶ Wednesday in Holy Week, 10th April, 1566.

⁷ Palm Sunday, 7th April, 1566.

⁸ Parker's *Correspondence* (PS), p. 275 ; Strype, *Parker*, i, p. 426 ; see
the list of preachers for that Lent, ibid, iii, p. 247.

eastern district of England (the dioceses of Canterbury, Rochester, Winchester and Chichester) in the Royal Visitation of the summer of 1559.[1] He is next mentioned in a writ dated 23rd January, 1559-60, concerning the presentation to a benefice in the diocese of Winchester, the affairs of which, pending the appointment of a new bishop, were being dealt with by Canterbury. With others, he acted on behalf of the Primate in the proceedings at which the right of presentation was confirmed to the patrons.[2] On 18th September, 1561, Becon was again commissioned by Parker, this time to visit, with two other prebendaries, the Hospital of Eastbridge at Canterbury ; the visitation was to take place on 26th October between the hours of eight and ten in the morning, and a report was to be made on the state of affairs at the Hospital.[3]

Becon is also named in a mandate issued by the Archbishop to the Dean and Chapter of Canterbury on 19th September, 1560,[4] presumably in connexion with the visitation of the Cathedral which was held about that time in the Chapter House.[5] On this occasion there were complaints of the neglect of Divine Service, and of drunkenness and unseemly behaviour among the Petty Canons, whose numbers were depleted. Women suspiciously resorted to the houses of certain clergy, and Reginald Pole's arms and cardinal's hat still hung in the Cathedral, which was " not decent, nor tolerable, but abominable, and not to be suffered".[6] Becon may well have had in mind the scandals going on around him when he wrote in the preface to the folio edition of his works a long indictment of the character of many of the ministers of the Church.[7]

In June or July of the following year the Primate required the bishops of the Province of Canterbury to furnish him with certificates in respect of each clergyman in their dioceses, and Strype fortunately selects as a specimen that relating to Becon, which runs :

[1] See H. Gee, *The Elizabethan Clergy* . . ., p. 101.
[2] Parker's *Register*, pp. 203-205.
[3] ibid, pp. 380-282 ; also Strype, *Parker*, i, pp. 202-203 ; a further visitation was made in 1569, and reforms were effected, ibid, pp. 565-566.
[4] Parker's *Register*, p. 631.
[5] Strype, *Parker*, i, pp. 144 ff.
[6] ibid, pp. 148-149.
[7] P i, pp. 5-6.

H

Eccles. Christi. | Mr. Becon, Vicar. Baccalaur. Art. | Presbyter Conjugatus | Doctus | Non residet | Degit Cantuar, interdum apud S. Stephan. Lond. | Praedicat, Licentiatus | Sacerdotia duo habet, istud et S. Stephan. in Walbrook | [1]

II

Between 1559 and 1563 much of Becon's time must have been occupied in preparing for the press the collected or folio edition of his works, which he undertook " at the instant desire of certain godly and zealous brethren", and for the printing of which a licence had been issued to John Day on 14th May, 1560.[2]

First, the pseudonymous writings brought out during Henry's reign were " revised and diligently perused", alterations being made where necessary to bring them into closer conformity with contemporary opinion.[3] The short metrical *Catechism* was replaced by *A New Catechism*, which occupies over four hundred pages of the Parker Society edition, and is less a catechism than a compendium of divinity in the form of a dialogue between a father and his precocious son who, not yet six years old, displays a wealth of theological erudition, a mature judgment, and a surprising knowledge of the world![4] To complete the first volume, which seems to have appeared in 1560, Becon wrote *The Book of Matrimony*, to which he prefixed the preface originally composed for the Bullinger-Coverdale treatise on marriage, altering nothing but the concluding paragraph. This is one of his most important works, though it suffers from a disproportionate concern with coarse anti-papal polemic, and with such unedifying matters as the supposed extent of sexual depravity among the mediaeval clergy and religious—both considerable items in the stock-in-trade of those who proclaimed the right of the minister to marry at his discretion.[5]

[1] Strype, *Parker*, i, p. 189.
[2] See E. Arber, *Transcript of the Register of the Company of Stationers of London*, i, p. 128 : " Recevyd of John Daye for his lycense for pryntinge of all Master Becon's works graunted the xiiij Daye of Maye, and he geveth to ye howse iij s iiij d."
[3] See Detached Note E for an example.
[4] For a further discussion of certain aspects of the *Catechism*, see Detached Note F.
[5] The *Book of Matrimony* is considered in more detail in chapter ix, § 11.

The second volume of the folio edition consists of Becon's Edwardine works, all previously published, and now reprinted with corrections. Of the works contained in the third volume, none had previously been issued in England,[1] though some of them had been published abroad. The *Comfortable Epistle* and the *Supplication* have already been noticed, but of the rest of the volume it is uncertain how much was written under Mary or in exile, and how much during Elizabeth's reign.

Reference has been made to *The Displaying of the Popish Mass*, which was probably written on the Continent, for Lowndes mentions a Latin edition published at Basel in 1559. In it, every vestment, every movement, every gesture, every word of the Mass is taken in turn and held up to ridicule, while the whole action is interpreted in a disparaging manner by means of a running commentary interspersed with disgusting innuendos. Its grossly blasphemous and indecent pages are reprinted by the Parker Society for those who wish to see to what foul and despicable uses the propagandist could lend his pen.

A comparison between the Lord's Supper and the Pope's Mass, a free rendering into English of the *Coenae . . . et Missae . . . Comparatio*, though in the style of the time, is less objectionable, but need not detain us. Its arguments and antitheses display no originality, but apparently the public for whom such literature was intended did not tire of its inordinate repetition, so long as the Mass and the Pope were being denounced.

Next may be mentioned two lesser-known works, omitted from the Parker Society edition—*The Relics of Rome*,[2] a catalogue of innovations in religion alleged to have been introduced by the Pope and " his adherents " ; and *The Monstrous Merchandise of the Romish Bishops*, an inventory of relics which may have been inspired by Calvin's *Admonitio de Reliquiis*.[3] Among the sources of this book Becon mentions

---

[1] See the table at the front of the folio edition.

[2] Dedicated to John Parkhurst, Bishop of Norwich, who writes to Foxe : " Commend me . . . to Mr. Day and his wife, and thank him for the book of the *Relics of Rome* which he sent me. I will thank Mr. Becon, which dedicated the same to my name, another time, if God so will." See Strype, *Annals*, I, ii, p. 46.

[3] *Opera*, viii, pp. 203-215 ; *cf* F iii, fol. clxxviii verso.

. . . an olde written boke, which is yet remayning in the Cathedral
church of Cantorburye . . . called *Memorale multorum, Henrici
Prioris*, and it may appeare by the accompte to be cclxii yeares
since it was written, and lefte for a perpetuall remembraunce of
such thinges as at that tyme appertayned unto the monasterye,
comõnly called Christes churche, being thē a place of monkes,
nowe thorowe the benefite & liberalitye of the most noble king
Henrye the eyght, a most worthy Cathedrall Church, and a place
of godly and learned Prebendaryes, &c. . . .[1]

He also made use of " The Reportes of certaine men, concerning
Rome, and the lewde behaviour vsed in the same", which
Strype seems to have regarded as a separate work.[2]

Among the *Reportes* is a recantation made by Dr. Richard
Smith, an eminent scholar and at heart a convinced Romanist,
though he twice abjured his opinions.[3] In one of his works,
*Confutatio eorum, quae Philippus Melanchthon obijcit contra
Missae sacrificium propitiatorium*,[4] Smith assailed Becon on
account of

. . . vanissima quaedam nugamenta et mera somnia . . . que ille
libro suo, cui titulum praeficit, de reliquiis Romae, non tam
imperite et impudenter, quam impie effutivit.[5]

and declared that " libellus . . . tuus, Beacone . . . nihil fere
complectitur praeter splendida mendacia". To this Becon
replied in the preface to the *Monstrous Merchandise*. . . . He
denounces Smith for a

. . . doubler dissembler and ranke Papiste . . . a suttle sicophant
and blasphemous backbiters of other mennes godly trauayles,
liuing in Brabant[6] as an ennemye of his owne natiue countrye
and an extreme aduersarye of Goddes true religion and of the
Quenes highnesses mooste godlye and lawfull proceedinges. . .

He wastes no time in refuting Smith's refutation, and concludes
with a characteristic malediction :

. . . better had it bene for him neuer to haue knowne the waye

---

[1] F iii, fol. clxxxxii verso.

[2] *Cranmer*, i, p. 244 ; Tanner, *Bibliotheca*, p. 85, also treats it as a separate
work : " Liber hic . . . Thomae nostro attribuitur " ; he had apparently not
realized that it was to be found in the folio edition as part of the *Monstrous
Merchandise*. . . .

[3] See D.N.B. Strype prints the first recantation from Becon's *Reportes*,
Cranmer, ii, pp. 795-799.

[4] Louvain, 1562.

[5] fol. 57 verso—58 recto.

[6] Smith was Dean of St. Peter's church, Douay, Chancellor of the
University, and Professor of Theology.

of righteousnesse, then after his knowledge, thus Jewdaslike to goo away from it, and not onlye to goo away from it, but also to persecute it, to blaspheme it, to wryte against it &c.   Verely great is his dampnation, except he spedely repent. . . .[1]

Among these later works are two more collections of probations, a favourite form of composition with Becon.   One is scriptural—*The Commonplaces of the holy scripture*, dedicated to his

. . . dear countrymen and faithful ministers of the Gospel of Jesu Christ, watching and attending upon the Lord's flock in the parishes of Norfolk and Suffolk.[2]

and the other patristic—*Certain Articles of Christian Religion*, dedicated to Grindal.   There is also a harmony of the four Gospels, *Christ's Chronicle*, and a *Summary of the New Testament*, an analysis of each book, chapter by chapter, inscribed to Thomas Moore, parson of Wethringset, to whose diligence and good example " known more than these twenty-four years " Becon pays tribute,[3] acknowledging his constancy during the late " cruel and bloody times".   *The Demands of Holy Scripture*, really two books in one, is a sort of catechism ; in the dedication to the " Mayor and his Brethren of Sandwich in Kent " Becon explains that the purpose of the work is " to help forward some point of godly doctrine to be taught in your new-erected school "—Sandwich School, which had just been founded.[4] *The Diversity between God's word and man's invention* and *The Acts of Christ and of Antichrist* are both lists of comparisons in which protestant principles are extolled and Romish practices and teachings condemned ;   the *Diversity* appears to be a free version of Francois Lambert's *Antithesis verbi dei et inventorum hominum*.   Two short compositions, *The Glorious Triumph of God's most blessed word*, inscribed to Archbishop Parker

. . . as a testimonie of my seruiceable hearte and faithful obedience towarde your honour, not hauyng otherwise wherewith in any poynt to shewe my thanckfull mynde towarde your grace, whiche hathe so oft and so many wayes most liberally deserued of me . . . ,[5]

---

[1] F iii, fol. clxxx. Strype mentions this passage between Smith and Becon in *Cranmer*, i, p. 609.

[2] P iii, p. 290.

[3] P iii, p. 566 ; *cf* p. 563.

[4] Preface dated 1st September, 1563 ; P iii, p. 601.

[5] F iii, fol. cccclxx verso.

and a dialogue between Man and Reason entitled *The Praise of Death*, conclude the third volume of Becon's collected works, which was published at the beginning of 1564. The lengthy preface, dated 17th January, 1563-4,[1] carries a dedication to the archbishops and bishops of the English Church, acquaints them with its condition, and urges them to stir up the gift that is in them, and complete the work of reformation.

Only one more work came from Becon's pen before he laid it down for ever—the *New Postil*, a collection of " honest plain sermons " upon the Sunday and Holy Day Gospels. There seems to be no evidence for Strype's statement that these discourses appear to be " only a translation either out of Latin or Dutch [German]".[2] The *New Postil* went into a second edition in the year following its publication, and affords a fitting close to the literary labours of one who was both diligent and respected as a preacher.

III

The Act of Uniformity and the Prayer Book of 1559, and the *Interpretations* put forth by the bishops to explain the references to vestments in the Royal Injunctions,[3] marked a revival of the controversy which had raged in Frankfort, and both ceremonies and vestments figured prominently in the proceedings of the Convocation which met on 13th January, 1562-3. After the rejection of one petition asking for reforms, another, in similar terms, was brought forward on 13th February, to which Becon appended his signature. It demanded the abrogation of holydays other than Sundays and principal feasts of Christ, the reading of divine service facing the people, the omission of the sign of the cross in baptism, " that the order of kneeling may be left to the discretion of the ordinary within his jurisdiction", that the surplice should be regarded as a sufficient vestment for the minister, and " that the use of organs be removed".[4] After a heated discussion these propositions were rejected, whereupon a third petition came from

---

[1] On this date, see Detached Note D (I).
[2] *Parker*, i, pp. 454-455.
[3] See W. M. Kennedy, *The Interpretations of the Bishops*.
[4] Strype, *Annals*, I, i, pp. 502-503.

8434

the lower house containing twenty-one articles and subscribed
by sixty-four members, the first signature being Becon's. Five
of the articles are interesting, since they throw further light
upon his views at this time :

III. That no private baptism be ministered hereafter, but only
by those that be ministers of the church.

IV. That in public baptism, the father of the infant (if he possibly
may) be present : and that he, and the godfathers and godmothers,
shall openly profess, and recite the articles of the Christian faith,
commonly called the Creed, and desire that the infant may in
that faith be baptized, and received into the church of Christ.
And they shall not answer in the infant's name to such questions
as heretofore have been demanded of them in that behalf.

V. That it may be added to the confession which is used to be
made before the ministration of the holy communion, that the
communicants do detest and renounce the idolatrous mass.

VI. That no person abide within the church during the time of the
communion, unless he do communicate. That is, they shall depart
immediately after the exhortation be ended, and before the
confession of the communicants.

VII. That all images of the Trinity and of the Holy Ghost be
defaced ; and that roods and all other images, that have been, or
hereafter may be superstitiously abused, be taken away out of all
places, public and private, and utterly destroyed.[1]

It is clear that not all who supported these petitions were
committed to the policy of the extremists. Some, for instance,
who voted against the second, subscribed the third. Not a few
desired further progress in the direction of moderate reform,
but would have been content to make concessions and to halt
short of the objectives proposed by the radicals, and of these
it seems that Becon was one. Fully in sympathy with some of
the Puritan ideals, and anxious to see certain changes in the
matter of ceremonies and vestments, he held nevertheless to
the opinion which he had endorsed at Frankfort, that the
practices of which the advanced party complained were " in
their own nature indifferent". If, therefore, for the sake of
edification it seemed expedient either to retain or to abolish
them, then within reasonable limits he was prepared to concur
—though for his own part he would prefer to see further
reforms effected. Most of the changes demanded by the
petitioners in Convocation had, in fact, already been conceded

[1] Strype, *Annals*, I, i, p. 508.

by the Coxians to Whittingham—but solely in the interest of
peace and quietness, and not because the ceremonies or usages
themselves were in any sense " impure or papistical". So far
Becon had gone then, and so far he would go again.

As one of the London incumbents, he was involved a year
later in the proceedings taken by Grindal to enforce uniformity
in his diocese. It seems that at first he refused to conform to
the wearing of the prescribed habits, and to observe the
ornaments rubric, the Royal Injunctions, and " the Book of
Convocation".[1] Later, however, with Whittingham, he subscribed and, according to Strype, was preferred. Strype goes on
to say that Becon " had Walbroke and another benefice in
London",[2] which is not, of course, correct ; he had by this time
resigned St. Stephen's and was in possession of St. Dionis
Backchurch and Christ Church, Newgate. He received no
subsequent preferment.

Later in the same year Parker asked for an assurance that
his own cathedral church was conforming to the rites and
ceremonies ordered by the Prayer Book. A certificate was
accordingly furnished to the Archbishop's Commissary, and to
it Becon, as one of the prebendaries, set his hand.[3] This
certificate shows that for the Daily Service the Communion
Table was set north and south, the officiant standing at the
east side in a surplice, facing the people. The Communion was
administered on the first Sunday of every month, the Table
then being set east and west ; the celebrant, epistoler, and
gospeller wore copes, and none but communicants were allowed
to remain in the chancel. When the prebendaries preached,
they were habited in surplice and silk hood.[4]

This confirms Becon's adiaphorism in the matter of ceremonies ; he certainly seems to have had no objection to
wearing in the cathedral at Canterbury the vestments there
in use. His conformity at Lambeth, after refusing to submit,
cannot be attributed to vacillation. He felt it right at the time

[1] The last named was a new draft of thirty-eight articles prepared from
the XLII Articles, and issued in English with one addition as the XXXIX
Articles of 1571.
[2] Strype, *Grindal*, p. 145.
[3] He signs here, Thomas Beacon.
[4] Strype, *Parker*, i, pp. 364-366 has the certificate in full.

to withhold his subscription, but later, having considered the matter and understanding that no question of principle was involved, he did not hesitate to submit.

In the *New Catechism* he affirms his view that " gestures are free, so that none occasion of evil be either done or offered ",[1] and concludes that

> . . . if a magistrate, being godly, command that the minister in the time of his administration wear a surplice, not for the maintenance of superstition, but for a seemly and decent order, his commandment in this behalf is to be obeyed, and no godly minister ought to resist it. . . . But in things that be indifferent, we must take heed that we clog no man's conscience, nor make that a thing of necessity which is mere voluntary.[2]

Becon makes very few other references to vestments, and obviously did not regard them as important in themselves. In the preface to the folio edition there is a passage in which he enlarges upon the symbolism of the Elizabethan bishop's rochet and chimere.[3]

IV

Becon's last years were quiet and on the whole uneventful. He seems to have resided for the most part in his prebendal house at Canterbury, under the shadow of the great cathedral, except when preaching took him away, or when the affairs of one of his benefices required his attention. Occupied in daily attendance at the Common Prayer in the choir, in chapter business, and in study, writing, and the revision of his works, he passed these eight years peacefully and congenially. His health does not appear to have been good, and this may have disinclined him to enter more actively into ecclesiastical and public affairs ; it may also account for the fact that he received no further preferment of consequence after his prebendal stall. He describes *The Book of Matrimony* as " the frute of my labours and paynes in my late and long sickenes ",[4] and this may be the illness to which he refers in an undated letter to

[1] P ii, p. 299.
[2] P ii, p. 300.
[3] See P i, p. 31.
[4] F i, fol. cccclxvi verso.

Parker, which appears to be the only manuscript of his now extant :[1]

My moste humble dutie consydered towarde youre grace : it maye | please youre Honoure to vnderstande, that as it greatly delyghted me | to heare of youre graces prosperous returne into thys contrye, whyche | (I doubte not) shall be greatly bothe vnto ye glorye of God and vnto | the profytt of hys people, so lykewyse it not a lyttle greued me, that | hytherto thorowe certayne infirmities and diseases, wherewythe I haue | bene troubled more then thys half yeare at certayne tymes vnto y^e | greate losse of my tyme and hyndrauns of my studies, I coulde not | attende vpon youre grace accordyng to my dutie. But to declare in the | meane season my seruiseable and faythefull hearte towarde youre Ho | noure, I send vnto youre grace an olde monument worthy to be pre | serued and embrased for ye antiquities sake, namely, an exposicion | vpon ye Gospelles of S.Marcke, and of S. Luke, wythe all ye Epistles | of S. Paule bothe in Latin and Englyshe : whereunto my wyffe | youre Graces daly Oratrix hathe added hyr poore present, that is a | couple of fatte capons and syx chykyns, bothe of vs moste entierly wyshyng | from God vnto youre Grace, continuall healthe and prosperous felicitie, | wythe dayly encrease of honoure.   From youre Graces Metropoliticall | Churche at Cantorburye thys present Wednysdaye.

youre Graces moste humble :

Tho. Becon.

At the comparatively early age of fifty-five Becon died at his home in Canterbury on 30th June, 1567.[2]   There is no record of his burial, which probably took place in the city, if not in the cathedral itself.[3]

---

[1] Corpus Christi College, Cambridge, MSS ; in M. R. James's Catalogue, item 302 in MS 114.

[2] Parker's *Register*, p. 525 ; *cf* pp. 833 and 834 ; also le Neve, *Fasti*, i, p. 50. There is no foundation for the statement, to be found in works of reference and elsewhere, that Becon died in 1570 at the age of 60.

[3] The cathedral burial records do not begin until 1570, and the burial registers of other Canterbury churches contain no reference to Becon's burial.

My moste humble dutie remembred towardes your Grace: it may
please your Honoure to vnderstande, that as it greatly delighted me
to heare of your Graces prosperous returne into thys contrey, which
I doubte not shall be greatly bothe vnto the glorye of god and vnto
the proffett of hys people, so likewise is it not a litle greiud me, that
by those thoughe strange infirmities and diseases, wherwithe I haue
bene troubled more than this halfe yeare at certayne tymes, vnto the
greate losse of my tyme and hyndrance of my studies, I coulde not
attende vpon your Grace accordyng to my dutie. But to declare in the
meane season my seruiceable and faythfull hearte towarde your Honoure, I send vnto your Grace an olde monument worthy to be pre-
serued and embraced for of antiquities sake, namely, an Exposition
vpon the Gospells of S. Marcke, and of S. Luke; with the all the Epistles
of S. Paule bothe in Latin and Englyshe: Whervnto my desire
your Graces dayly Oratour hathe added for youe present, that is a
couple of fatte capons, and six chystyng, bothe of his moste entirely wyshyng
from god vnto your Grace continuall healthe and prosperous felicitie
withe dayly encrease of honoure. From your Graces Metropoliticall
Churche of Canterburye this present Wednysdaye.

your Graces moste humble

Tho. Broon

CHAPTER IX

THOMAS BECON THE REFORMER

IN estimating Becon's teaching and opinions it must not be forgotten that he was primarily not a theologian but a propagandist, and that he was never involved in any controversy of such a nature as to necessitate his advancing or defending a precise doctrinal position. Many of his views have been discussed in the course of this study, but nothing has been said of his teaching on the Church, the sacraments, and marriage, and I propose to deal with each of these briefly in turn. It appears from an examination of his " first period " writings and his second recantation that during Henry's reign Lutheranism was the dominant influence in his theology, but after 1548 he seems to have adopted Zwinglian views, and to have retained these, with perhaps a little modification in a Calvinistic direction, until the end of his life.

I

Becon says very little about the doctrine of the Church, but the two passages following give some indication of his views :

> . . . I confess that to be the holy catholic and apostolic church which is the company and fellowship of the saints, that is to say, of the faithful, which are sanctified and made holy by the Spirit of God, and by the blood of Christ our Saviour ; which have the pure word of God truly and sincerely preached, and the sacraments duly and faithfully ministered among them ; which excommunicate all disobedient notable sinners, and receive into their fellowship such as unfeignedly repent and turn from their wickedness, which study in all things to please the Lord God, and to live " in all godliness and honesty".[1]

[1] *The Sick Man's Salve*, P iii, p. 143.

The true Church

> . . . is that holy congregation or fellowship of God's elect, which
> cannot err, nor be brought into error, much less perish and be
> damned. . . .

Its " notes " are

> . . . the sincere, true, and uncorrupt preaching of God's word,
> without the intermixtion or mingling of man's doctrine . . . the
> true administration of the sacraments according to the institution
> and ordinance of Christ . . . fervent prayer and the diligent
> invocation of God in the name of our alone Mediator, Jesus
> Christ, with continual thanksgiving for his benefits . . . ecclesi-
> astical discipline according to the prescript and appointment of
> God's word. . . .

and it is " ' catholic ' or universal " because it is dispersed
throughout the whole world.[1]

There are here unmistakeable affinities with Calvinist
doctrine, but Becon's teaching on the sacraments is distinctly
Zwinglian, at least to the extent that, like his master Cranmer,
his thought, especially in connexion with the Eucharist,
" moved within the basic framework of Zwingli's opinions".[2]

The sacraments, he says, are outward signs or tokens of
membership of the true Church and of a Christian man's
profession ; pledges of God's mercy, grace, and favour ;
reminders of that charity which ought to be between the
followers of the Lord ; and testimonials

> . . . to testify and witness how nigh Christ join[s] himself unto us,
> that he giveth himself whole unto us, and that he will dwell in
> us, and endow us with all his benefits and riches, so that what-
> soever is Christ's, the same is ours.[3]

But he expressly asserts that

> . . . the sacraments by themselves and by their own power do
> not give grace, nor the Spirit of God, neither justify the receiver.[4]

---

[1] *A New Catechism*, P ii, p. 42.

[2] C. C. Richardson, *Zwingli and Cranmer on the Eucharist* [*Cranmer Dixit
et Contradixit*], p. 48. Dr. Richardson's lecture contains an admirable and
very important examination of the real nature of Zwingli's teaching, and
answers the question, Was Cranmer a Zwinglian ? He also discusses the
points at issue between Mr. G. B. Timms (*Dixit Cranmer, Church Quarterly
Review*, Jan.-March and April-June, 1947) and Dom Gregory Dix (*Dixit
Cranmer et Non Timuit*, ibid, Jan.-March and April-June, 1948).

[3] *A New Catechism*, P ii, p. 201.

[4] ibid, P ii, pp. 218-219 ; *cf* the preface to the folio edition, P i, p. 12, and
Certain Articles of Christian Religion, no. XVI, P iii, p. 466, &c.

When, therefore, he says :

> . . . partaking of our Lord Jesus Christ is given to us through the word and the signs instituted for this purpose of God.[1]

he does not mean that preaching and the Communion, for example, are means whereby Christ is received in any " substantial " manner ; they simply provide the occasion when the divine presence of Christ can be grasped by the faithful heart. Although to the appointed outward sign there is annexed a promise of grace, the reception of that grace depends entirely upon faith, which he defines in true Reformation terms as a

> . . . certain, assured, and an undoubted persuasion of the mind, *conceived of the word of God through the operation of the Holy Ghost* concerning the performance and enjoyment of such heavenly things as God hath promised in his holy scriptures to the faithful.[2]

In other words, faith is primarily an act of the Holy Spirit through which man is brought into a new relation with Christ by which Christ dwells in the soul ; it is not merely an attitude of mind.

Becon teaches that baptism with the Holy Spirit is prior to baptism with water, which simply testifies to the congregation that the person baptized has already been regenerated and incorporated into the Body of Christ. He holds that the children of believers, like those of the Israelites, receive the Holy Spirit " even in their mother's womb", and, having been given " the best and chiefest baptism", may not be denied the other : " God hath baptized them with the Holy Ghost ; and shall we disdain to baptize them with water ?"[3] He denounces the " madness of those apish anabaptists",[4] and will not refuse baptism to infants who, pleasing God, must necessarily have faith[5] ; nor will he allow that want of water-baptism annuls the election of God. Jesus' saying : " Except a man be born of water and the Spirit, he cannot enter into the kingdom of

---

[1] *Catechism*, P ii, p. 199.
[2] *A New Catechism*, P ii, p. 13, my italics.
[3] ibid, P ii, p. 208.
[4] ibid, P ii, p. 209.
[5] ibid, P ii, p. 212 ; Becon proves this by means of the syllogism : Without faith it is impossible to please God (Heb. xi. 6) ; but children do please God ; therefore children must have faith !

God " must be understood as referring only to those who contemptuously refuse the ordinances of Christ.[1]

We do not know the nature of the offensive preaching against the Sacrament of the Altar to which Becon confesses in his first recantation, but in *A Christmas Banquet* there occurs a remarkable passage, of which it is surprising that no retraction was demanded in 1543. It will be remembered that *Philemon* had inscribed on his dishes the text, John vi. 53b-56[2] ; this, he says,

> . . . putteth us in remembrance, when we eat our meat, of the breaking of Christ's most blessed body and the shedding of his most precious blood ; and by the remembrance of it, and the believing of the same, our souls at that very present are no less fed and sustained than our bodies are with the meat that is brought unto us in these dishes.[3]

The exact import of this is not clear ; if Becon had in 1542 adopted the idea that every meal was in some sense a Communion, he soon abandoned it, for there is no hint of it in any later work.

Becon's Zwinglianism emerges clearly in an early Edwardine work, *The Flower of Godly Prayers*. A prayer before the reception of the Sacrament runs :

> . . . as thou didst ennoble the bread with the name of thy body, being but the figure of thy body because the breaking of thy body should the better be remembered ; so likewise here dost thou garnish and nobly set forth the wine, naming it thy blood, when, notwithstanding, it only representeth and preacheth unto us the shedding of thy blood. . . . O most merciful Redeemer and gentle Saviour, we are come together at this present to celebrate the memorial of thy blessed and glorious passion, and to eat and drink this bread and wine in the remembrance of thy body-breaking and blood-shedding. . . .[4]

The communicant takes the bread with thanksgiving, " in remembrance " of the sacrifice of the cross, and as he receives the cup, prays :

> In remembrance of this so noble a victory and of so great a benefit, I am come unto this thy table, O merciful Father, to drink of this cup, desiring thee, that as my outward man is

[1] *A New Catechism*, P ii, p. 224.
[2] See above, p. 25.
[3] P i, p. 65.
  P iii, p. 54.

comforted by the drinking of this wine, so likewise my inward
man may be comforted and made strong by true faith in the
precious blood of thy most dearly [beloved] Son.[1]

The thanksgiving after Communion refers to the Eucharist as

. . . a blessed memorial of [Christ's] death and passion, set forth
in the holy bread and holy wine, which we at this present have
received, both for a remembrance of the breaking of his blessed
body and the shedding of his most precious blood, and also for
the quietness of our conscience, and for the assurance of the
remission of our sins through faith.[2]

Similar views are expressed in other works of this period,[3]
and even in the *Demands of Holy Scripture*, written in 1563,[4]
while the *New Catechism* recalls Zwingli's conception of the
sacramental elements as *signa representativa*, though like him
it also speaks of a real nourishment of the soul by Christ
received through faith ; the bread and wine are

. . . figures, which by Christ's institution be unto the godly
receivers thereof sacraments, tokens, significations, and represen-
tations of his very flesh and blood ; instructing their faith, that as
the bread and wine feed them corporally, and continue this
temporal life ; so the very flesh and blood of Christ feedeth them
spiritually, and giveth everlasting life.[5]

Becon is thoroughly Zwinglian in the *New Catechism*, when
he affirms the ubiquity of Christ's spiritual or divine presence
while denying the ubiquity of his glorified Body ;[6] when he
rejects the view that the ungodly receive the Lord's Body and
Blood spiritually in the Sacrament ;[7] and when he states
expressly that the Lord's Supper was instituted to be

. . . an holy memorial and worthy remembrance of [Christ's]
passion and death, of his body-breaking and blood-shedding. . . .

and also a

. . . sign and token of the unity and concord, of the hearty good
will and singular friendship, and of the perfect agreement in
doctrine and religion that ought to be among them that profess
Christ,

[1] P iii, p 56.
[2] P iii, p. 55.
[3] See P iii, p. 67, and *The Sick Man's Salve*, P iii, p. 125 ; also *A Humble
Supplication . . .*, P iii, pp. 230 and 241.
[4] P iii, p. 617.
[5] P ii, pp. 283-284.
[6] P ii, p. 272.
[7] P ii, p. 291.

as well as a means by which faith is confirmed, the soul nourished, and thanks returned to God for our salvation.[1] But there are other passages where, at first sight, it might seem that he goes beyond the Zurich doctrine in speaking of a real " substantial " eating and drinking, synchronous with the corporal reception of the bread and wine. In the Edwardine work, *The Principles of Christian Religion*, he says that the faithful

> . . . besides the corporal eating . . . and outward drinking . . . do spiritually through faith both eat the body of Christ and drink his blood, unto the confirmation of their faith, the comfort of their conscience, and the salvation of their souls.[2]

In *The Demands of Holy Scripture* this is even more explicit :

> . . . even as sure as we take the bread and eat it with the mouth of the body, and drink the wine, so verily and certainly, even at the same instant, with the mouth of our faith, we receive the very body and blood of Christ.[3]

It might appear from such statements that Becon had leanings towards Bucer's eucharistic doctrine that " while the mouth receives the bread and wine, the worthy soul receives and feeds upon the very body and blood of Christ".[4]   This, however, would be to assume that for Becon, " spiritual " eating and drinking with the " mouth of faith" meant partaking of Christ " substantially", whereas there is no evidence that he differed from Zwingli and Cranmer in understanding it to denote simply a relationship with Christ through faith in the Passion.   If there were any doubt about his view, this passage from the *New Catechism* should dispel it :

> . . . Christ is eaten or received two manner of ways ; that is to say, sacramentally and spiritually.   He is received or eaten sacra- mentally, when we eat and drink the sacramental bread and wine, according to the institution of Christ ; which thing is done not only of the faithful, but also of the unfaithful.   He is also eaten or received spiritually, when we believe in Christ, embrace him as

---

[1] P ii, pp. 229-231.
[2] P ii, pp. 508-509.
[3] P iii, pp. 612-613.
[4] C. H. Smyth, *Cranmer and the Reformation under Edward VI*, p. 24 ; see also pp. 23-25 (it is unnecessary now to point out that this doctrine is incorrectly termed " Suvermerianism "), and C. Hopf, *Martin Bucer and the English Reformation*, pp. 41-51.

our alone Saviour, put our whole hope, trust, and confidence of our redemption and salvation in that one and alone sacrifice, which Christ offered upon the altar of the cross. . . .[1]

In his doctrine of the Eucharist, Becon was basically a Zwinglian, but it is impossible to say whether or not he adopted Cranmer's modifications of Zwingli's teaching.[2]

II

Becon's treatment of marriage falls into three parts. Like the rest of the reformers, he deals at inordinate length with compulsory celibacy and the abuses and immorality it was held to have occasioned among clergy, monks and nuns, illustrating his theme with racy but unedifying instances of mediaeval licentiousness. These passages need not detain us ; their aim is solely polemical. It suited his purpose to vituperate the catholic priests and religious and to paint them as libertines, and the slander is too impudent to need refutation. There were abuses and immorality, but Becon's sweeping denunciations of clerical " whoremongers " is grossly unfair, especially when directed against the legitimized cohabitations which, in all but their regularity, were often true marriages.[3]

Becon also treats at length of the duties and obligations of the married state, taking as his starting-point the " social codes " in the Ephesian, Colossian, Pastoral, and first Petrine Epistles,[4] and making use of appropriate *exempla* from the Old Testament. These exhortations to husband and wife are formal and thoroughly conventional, entirely androcentric, and based upon a one-sided interpretation of the Pauline doctrine of subordination. Woman is the inferior, and should in all things submit to her husband and be guided and ruled by him,[5]

---

[1] P ii, p. 294.

[2] See C. C. Richardson, *op. cit.* Darwell Stone observes that Becon " appears to have wavered between Virtualism, such as that held by Cranmer, and the Zwinglian opinion that the Sacrament is merely symbolical of Christ " (*The Doctrine of the Holy Eucharist*, ii, p. 235), but Dr. Richardson points out that Cranmer was not a Virtualist, in Stone's sense (*op. cit.*, pp. 32-33).

[3] *cf* Zwingli's " marriage " ; see T. M. Lindsay, *History of the Reformation*, ii, pp. 36-37.

[4] See E. G. Selwyn, *The First Epistle of St. Peter*, pp. 419 ff.

[5] *A New Catechism*, P ii, p. 340.

bearing patiently with his faults and incommodities.[1]   But
Becon does not condone the latter ; he denounces the " currish
and doggish behaviour of some loosebands, rather than hus-
bands "[2] who forget that

> . . . their wives be no dish-clouts, nor no handbasket-sloys, nor
> no drudges, nor yet slavish people, but fellow-heirs with them of
> everlasting life.

and, moreover, often so wise and prudent in daily affairs that
they can

> . . . many times . . . give better counsel than men, and are able
> to determine what is good and what is otherwise, no less than their
> husbands.[3]

Against the traditional view of woman, still at that time widely
current despite " romantic " influences, he asserts that

> . . . the blessed trinitie is the creatour and maker no les of the
> woman, than of the man : whereby it is geuen us to vnderstande,
> that the woman is before God of no less price and dignitie, then
> man is, so that they which so contemptuously and so despitefully
> either write or speak of the feminine kind, do great dishonour to
> God.[4]

But the most important and original parts of the *Book of
Matrimony*, Becon's largest work on the subject, are those
which deal with the theological aspects of the marriage union.
This composition is not, however, a systematic treatise ; its
main purpose is polemical and hortatory, and it must not be
forgotten that it was written for and dedicated to Thomas
Wotton, and treats of the duties and practical problems of
married life chiefly from the husband's standpoint. Nor does
it lack the inconsistency to be found in the matrimonial
treatises of most Reformation and Caroline divines. At one
moment Becon is the theologian expounding a conventional
view of sexual relation and marriage ;[5] at another he is the
husband and father, drawing upon a rich experience of married
and family life.

[1] *A New Catechism*, P ii, p. 343.
[2] ibid, P ii, p. 338.
[3] ibid, P ii, p. 339.
[4] *The Book of Matrimony*, F i, fol. cccclxix recto.
[5] Despite the changes introduced by the reformers into the concept of
Christian marriage, it is often overlooked that protestantism took over, and
even exaggerated, certain traditional views of sexual relation.

For Becon marriage is a vocation ; it is not

> . . . brought to passe by fortune or by chaunce, but by the singular providence : determinacion : councel : wysedom : and tofore appoyntmente of God : according to this our common prouerbe. Matrimony is destinye.[1]

Men and women are drawn together " by a certain inspiration of the Holy Ghost",[2] by whom love is engrafted in their hearts.[3] Marriage excels every other state in life,[4] a conviction which Becon defends with great vigour and enthusiasm. In this, he is one of a minority of extremists among the reformers ; most of them were prepared to allow that voluntary virginity is superior to, or at least no less meritorious than marriage,[5] and on the strength of St. Paul's preference, conceded that in some cases it could have real value. Becon, too, would not deprive of their Christian liberty those who possess the gift of continency and elect to remain celibate,[6] but he holds that in exercising their choice they reject the higher state and prefer the lower.

For the three *bona matrimonii* of the Augustinian-Thomist theory of marriage (*fides, proles, sacramentum*) the English reformers substituted the three " causes for which matrimony was ordained "—procreation, a remedy against sin, and mutual society, help and comfort. There is no general agreement among them, however, as to the order in which these " causes " should be placed. Only the abortive *Reformatio Legum Ecclesiasticarum* follows the Prayer Book order stated above ;[7] Tyndale reverses it ;[8] but the majority of the reformers favour

---

[1] *The Book of Matrimony*, F i, fol. cccclxix recto.

[2] Preface to *The Book of Matrimony*, F i, fol. cccclxii verso (*The Christian State of Matrimony*, A iii, verso).

[3] *A New Catechism*, P ii, p. 341.

[4] *The Book of Matrimony*, fol. Dcxvi verso ; *cf* Preface (ibid, F i, fol· cccclxii recto : *The Christian State of Matrimony*, fol. A ii recto—A iv recto)·

[5] See, e.g., Hutchinson, *The Image of God*, xxv (*Works* [PS], p. 148) ; Latimer, *Sermons* (PS), p. 394 ; Fulke, *Defence of the English Translation of the Bible*, xvi, § 1 (*Works* [PS], p. 492) ; *Stapleton's Fortress Overthrown*, II, *Answers* (PS), p. 99.

[6] *A New Catechism*, P ii, p. 103.

[7] *de matrimonia*, i ; see Cardwell's ed., p. 39.

[8] *The Obedience of a Christian Man*, *Works* (PS), i, p. 254.

society ; procreation ; remedy ;[1] and Becon agrees with the general view.[2]

In the case of adultery, Becon holds that the marriage union is dissolved,[3] yet not so absolutely as to preclude reinstatement of the offending partner after due repentance,[4] and he pleads for reconciliation and reunion wherever possible.[5] In permitting divorce only in the event of adultery he is more conservative than many of his contemporaries ;[6] like them, however, on the authority of the traditional exegesis of Matthew xix. 9,[7] he would allow the remarriage of a guiltless person lawfully divorced.[8]

Sometimes the husband forgets that he is a theologian, as when he descants upon the theme, " Matrimoni all loue " :[9]

The wiues loue is with no falsity corrupted, with no simulation abscured, with no chaūce of things minished. Finally with death only (nay not with death neither) withdrawn.. She, the loue of her parents : she, the loue of her sisters : she, the loue of her brethren despiseth for the loue of you : her only respect is to you : of you she hangeth : with you she coueteth to die. Haue ye richesse. There is one that shal saue it : there is one that shal encrease it. Haue ye none : there is one that may seke it : if ye haue wealth, your felicity is doubled. If aduersity, there shalbe one, which may comfort you, which may sit by your side, which may serue you, which may couet your grefe to be hers. Do ye iudge any pleasure to be compared with this so great a coniunction : If ye tary at home, there is at hand, which shal driue away the tediousness of solitarye being. If from home, ye haue one that shall kisse you, when ye depart : long for you, when ye be absent, receiue you ioyfully, when ye returne. A swete companion of youth, a kind solace of age. . . .

[1] See Hooper, *A Declaration of the Ten Commandments*, x, *Works* (PS), i, p. 381 ; Bucer, for whose view see Hopf, *op. cit.*, p. 72 ; Sandys, Sermon xvi, *Works* (PS), p. 315; also the Homily, *Of the State of Matrimony, Homilies*, p. 534.

[2] See *The Book of Matrimony*, F i, fol. Dcxlviii recto ff.; Dcl verso ff.; Dcliv verso ff.

[3] ibid, F i, fol. Dcxxvi verso.

[4] As Hooper would have wished. see *A Declaration of the Ten Commandments*, x, *Works* (PS), i, p. 384 ; *cf* ii, p. xxiii and *Orig. Let.*, p. 416.

[5] *The Book of Matrimony*, F i, fol. Dcxliii verso.

[6] e.g., Tyndale, *Exposition of Matt. v, vi, and vii*, on v. 31-32, *Works* (PS), ii, p. 55 ; also *Reformatio Legum Ecclesiasticarum, de adulteriis et divortiis*, 6, 9 and 11 ; *cf* 10.

[7] *The Book of Matrimony*, F i, fol. Dcxlii verso.

[8] ibid, F i, fol. Dcxxviii verso ; also *The Acts of Christ and of Antichrist* (of their doctrine), P iii, p. 532.

[9] It should not be forgotten that in this passage Becon is reminding a *husband* of the blessings of marriage and a good wife.

And to all this there can be added the blessing of children :

> Now sir, how highlye will ye esteme this thing, when your fair
> wife shal make you a father to a fair childe : when some litle
> yong babe shall play in your haull, which shall resemble you and
> your wife : which with a milde lisping, or amiable stammering
> shal call you Dad. . . .[1]

Here, in the words of one of the first of the English clergy to
judge that marriage would serve better to godliness, we catch
a glimpse of the spirit which has animated countless parsonages
—that ideal of Christian wedlock which has been, and still is,
Anglicanism's characteristic vindication of a married priesthood. It is regrettable that we know nothing of Becon's own
marriage, but something of its quality must surely be enshrined
in this and other passages in his works where he writes so
finely of the married state.

III

Although in neither events nor formularies can any certain
trace of his influence be detected, his biography shows that
Thomas Becon was undoubtedly a man of some consequence.
The story which has now been told confirms the opinion expressed in the Introduction, that he must be regarded as
notable among the English reformers for his work as a tract
writer and propagandist. If the opposition which his writings
provoked, and the ultimate success of the movement whose
principles he so strenuously advocated, are any measure of the
power of his pen, his contribution to the triumph of the
Reformation in England, though intangible, can by no means
be dismissed as negligible. Not only was he one of the most
voluminous of those who wrote in its support, but he was
certainly one of the most popular, and if we enquire the reason
for this, we shall find that it was, in some degree at least,
because his compositions had the qualities of their defects.

Becon's works are not, and were not intended to be, theological treatises, but as tracts for the times they are admirable.
Their simple, homely language and colloquial idiom, their many
proverbial sayings, their clarity of arrangement and statement

---

[1] *The Book of Matrimony*, F i, fol. Dcl.

and their effective *exempla*, show his genius for popular exposition and apologetic. While eschewing, as a general rule, any discussion of fine points of exegesis and doctrine, and relying upon direct and sometimes arresting assertions of protestant faith and teaching, he nevertheless amply furnishes his readers with the sort of arguments likely to be of most use to them—arguments against the Mass and transubstantiation, against the papal claims and jurisdiction, against superstitions, clerical celibacy, and so forth. He provides abundant ammunition for the ordinary protestant to fire at his Papist or temporizing neighbours, and reasons enough to confirm the wavering and doubtful and to encourage those already convinced. Not the least striking feature of his method is his use of scripture. Page after page abounds in quotation and allusion, skilfully woven into the argument. This had a double aim ; it guaranteed a scriptural sanction for his teaching, and it also served to familiarize the reader with the Bible and its contents, particularly when all but a few were forbidden to read it. And if it has to be admitted that perhaps not the least of the factors making for Becon's popularity was his outbursts of coarse vituperation and his command of all the alliterative and other devices of vulgar and abusive polemic, it must also be allowed that in this respect he was not alone or even pre-eminent in his age. His language, though sometimes regrettable, is moderate when compared with the worst of Bale, and he rarely descended to the level of the *Supplication* or *The Displaying of the Popish Mass.*

If Becon's greatest importance in the progress and success of the Reformation in England lies in his power and ability as a propagandist, there are other respects also in which he deserves to be recognized and remembered. Not least of these is his undoubted influence upon English protestant piety. Through most of his work there runs a note of deep personal devotion, tinged though it is with something of a puritanical severity and over-confidence of election and predestination to salvation. It is not surprising that so many of his prayers found a place in the Primer of 1553. They show little liturgical sense, and nothing of that beauty and felicity of phrase and structure which he must often have admired in the work of his master and patron, but they have a sincerity and directness which lends them a distinctive character. They must have been extensively used, and were no doubt as popular as some of his devotional works themselves. Although Becon's idea of prayer is dominated by petition to the virtual exclusion of its other aspects, the treatise *A New Pathway unto Prayer*, and the relevant section of the *New Catechism* contain much admirable matter written in a spirit of true understanding, and testifying to a real experience of communion with God, and an appreciation of the basic place of prayer in the Christian life. It is the more regrettable that into these devotional works, and even into the prayers themselves, the old prejudices and antipathies intrude, and that at any moment the Mass, the Pope, priests, purgatory, or some other King Charles's head may introduce a discordant and not infrequently vindictive note.

Becon has a value, too, for the historian. His works, as we have seen, are a mine of information about the social and economic conditions of his time, and about popular protestant opinion in England. If he wrote for the humbler supporters of the Reformation, he also reflected their views. In book after book we hear the echoes, not of debates in Convocation but of sermons at Paul's Cross and other well-frequented preaching places, not of theological discussion at the table of some prelate or Doctor, but of earnest talk and careful searchings of the scriptures as friends gather round the fireside or walk in the garden.

Neither in his life nor in his works do we find the consistency in action and thought of one whose mind is made up ; who has carefully worked out all his conclusions and stands secure, fortified by his own logic, in a position whence neither argument nor doubt nor persecution can dislodge him. Of some, like Hooper and Latimer, this could be said, but not of Becon. He was sensitive to the perplexities of his age ; he knew clearly on which side he stood—but exactly where on that side he was never entirely sure. And in this deeply-rooted uncertainty he reflects the uncertainty of many, perhaps of most of his contemporaries. In him is mirrored the ordinary protestant Englishman who, having taken a major decision, finds that all his problems are not thereby automatically solved. We in a different age know something of this natural hesitancy in the face of great and rapid change, this instinctive search for a *via media* amidst conflicting theories and rival claims, and it may help us to understand the bewilderment which must have assailed men four hundred years ago.

In this typical character Becon may afford us a clue to the ideas and conduct of others. Like many more, his roots struck deeper than he realized into the old traditions and ways. In his exaltation of the "powers that be" he is the thorough Erastian, yet he cannot deny that the Norfolk rebels have a case and a claim upon his sympathy, despite the sinfulness of riot and civil commotion, and he fully endorses the theory that when the "power" is a woman and a Romanist, there is a limit to the obedience of the subject. He is one of the few Englishmen to express a decided preference for sitting at the Communion, yet he holds that ceremonies and gestures in themselves are *adiaphora*; he is found with Cox at Frankfort when he might have been expected to side with Whittingham and the Knoxians; he moves and petitions in Convocation against vestments, yet at Canterbury he conforms to the local use of surplice and cope; he refuses to submit at Grindal's visitation, yet afterwards subscribes.

On a superficial view this might be attributed to vacillation and cowardice, as Jacobs does Becon's recantations and flights from danger. I believe, however, that it may more fairly be explained by this perplexity in the face of contradictory claims and ideas, which I have already mentioned. We see on the one hand a determination not to yield an inch in matters of principle, and on the other, a readiness to make concessions in things indifferent, an instinctive desire to discover the middle way between conflicting but not mutually exclusive points of view. In attempting to avoid an extreme and uncongenial position, Becon sometimes found himself uncertain where to take his stand. He himself makes much of the debt which he owed to Stafford and Latimer, but I believe that the dominant influence in his middle and later years was that of Cranmer, whose chaplain he had been, whose memory he revered, and whose ideals and principles he understood and took as his guide, both in exile and on his return to England. Impetuous and easily led, however, he sometimes found the moderate or middle path hard to discover, let alone to tread. Loyalty to the aims of his late master and patron not infrequently conflicted with a temperamental disposition to favour advanced views, and here, undoubtedly, an explanation of the inconsistencies of his later years must be sought.

By those historians who have noticed him, Becon has usually been numbered among the puritans, doubtless on the strength of his views on kneeling, his nonconformist tendencies (as seen in the 1562-3 Convocation and at Grindal's visitation), and the character of some of his works (notably those of a devotional nature). In his rigorist attitude to life and his severe piety there is indeed not a little that savours of the " puritanical " in the later sense of the word, and many features of the more extreme protestantism seem to have been congenial to him. But it is clear that he was not, strictly speaking, one of the early puritans, despite the efforts some of them seem to have made to claim him ; he was, for one thing, too moderate and adiaphoristic in the matter of gestures, ceremonies, and vestments. " Party " divisions, then or now, are never clear-cut, and the precise position of a non-extremist is often difficult to define. Despite certain superficial affinities with the puritan element in the English Church, no careful estimate of his life and works admits of Becon's being set down as a thorough-going puritan. Whether, had he lived, he would eventually have thrown in his lot with the advanced party, it is profitless to speculate.

CHAPTER X

THOMAS BECON THE WRITER

I

THIS study would be incomplete without a brief reference to Becon's literary aims and characteristics. Of the former, he himself writes :

. . . in all my sermons and writings I have not attempted matters of high knowledge and far removed from the common sense and capacity of the people, but I have been content at all times to handle such matters as might rather edify the brethren, than to drive them into an admiration or stupor at the doctrine of so rare, unwonted, high, and unsearchable mysteries, and as might most make unto the avancement of virtue and unto the repression of vice. . . .

To teach the people to know themselves and their salvation in the blood of Christ through faith, and to walk worthy of the kindness of God, leading a life agreeable to the same, hath only been the stop and mark whereunto I have directed all my studies and travails both in preaching and in writing.[1]

There is no doubt that he achieved these modest aims, but there can be no agreement with his remarks on the spirit in which he conducted controversy and treated his opponents :

I have sought in all my doings to offend none, but to please the godly. And therefore have I ever used a temperate, moderate, and quiet kind, both of preaching and of writing. . . .[2]

. . . I have not so dealt with the adversaries of God's true religion in any of my books, that I have at any time forgotten christian modesty, or passed the bounds of friendly peace. I have fought not with the men . . . but with their errors and wicked doctrines . . .[3]

. . . whatsoever I have written against the doctrine of antichrist in this third volume, I have not done it with uncharitable railings, cruel words, fiery invectives, taunting terms, unsavoury scoffings, uncomely jestings, &c., but with the authority of the holy scriptures, and with the testimonies of the godly ancient fathers,

[1] P i, pp. 27-28.
[2] P i, p. 28.
[3] P i, p. 29.

seeking all means possible to edify and not to destroy, to please and not to displease. . . .[1]

Upon so perverse an estimation of his own charity and good taste the *Supplication* and *The Displaying of the Popish Mass* provide the best commentary.

To great industry in composition Becon added a remarkable facility in expression and an intimate knowledge of the Bible. Although frequently marred by latinisms, especially in the early works, his style is fresh and vigorous, and at times exuberantly rhetorical. He is one of the most attractive and even entertaining writers among the English reformers ; like Latimer, whose preaching he greatly admired, he is homely and often colloquial, while popular idioms and proverbial expressions impart to his later compositions a telling and original flavour. More than any of his contemporaries he favoured the dialogue form for the purpose of propaganda and instruction, and the conversations between the four friends are natural and spirited.

Becon's writings are enlivened by many flashes of broad and sometimes vulgar humour, as well as by puns, alliterative abuse, and witticisms of all kinds. One example may suffice : the description of the priest's silent commemoration of the departed at the *Memento* in the Mass gives him full scope for his facetious propensities :

> And here in your mind and thought (for now ye play mum-budget and silence-glum) ye pray for Philip and Cheny, more than a good meany, for the souls of your great grand Sir and of your old beldam Hurre, for the souls of father Princhard and of mother Puddingwright, for the souls of good-man Rinsepitcher and good-wife Pintpot, for the souls of sir John Huslegoose and sir Simon Sweetlips. . . .[2]

Proverbs and proverbial sayings abound in his pages ; some have survived, but the majority are now obsolete. Here are a few of the more interesting :

> As soon to the market for to be sold
> Cometh the young sheep as the old.[3]

> Little wot the full sow, that is in the sty,
> What the hungry sow aileth, that goeth by.[4]

[1] P i, p. 30.
[2] P iii, p. 276.
[3] P iii, p. 118.
[4] P ii, p. 583.

It is merry in hall
When beards wag all.[1]

As riseth my good,
So riseth my blood.[2]

Every man before he dieth shall see the devil.[3]

Like will to like, quod the devil, when he danced
with the collier.[4]

Wherever God buildeth his church, there the devil also buildeth
his chapel.[5]

Summa Dei pietas veniam non dimidiabit ;
Aut nihil, aut totum, te poenitente dabit.[6]

Da tua, dum tua sunt : post mortem tunc tua non sunt.[7]

Quod sibi quisque serit praesentis tempore vitae,
Hoc sibi messis erit, cum dicitur, Ite, venite.[8]

Some of the sayings are quite obscure, but it is possible to
guess at the meaning of others :

of women who will not stay at home, but are always out on
pleasure bent—

Their house is a wild cat. They shall easily find it again at their
return. Set cock on the hoop. Let the devil pay the maltman.[9]

of the priest's manual actions at the Mass—

. . . play cole under candlestick . . . whip master Wynchard above
the board.[10]

of the elevation of the host—

. . . behold the apple-maker of Kent, and mark well him that
killed thy father.[11]

[1] P iii, p. 583.
[2] P ii, p. 599.
[3] P ii, p. 624.
[4] P iii, p. 383 ; cf P i, p. 132.
[5] P iii, p. 400.
[6] P ii, p. 174.
[7] P ii, p. 393 ; P iii, p. 128.
[8] ibid. These lines seem to have been taught in school (see P iii, p. 128),
and were doubtless familiar to Becon from his teaching. " Ite, venite " refers
to Matt. xxv. 34 and 41.
[9] P ii, p. 343 ; P iii, p. 282 ; see Oxford English Dict., s. vv. " wild-cat",
" cock-on-the-hoop", " maltman".
[10] P iii, p. 260 ; the phrase seems to denote secrecy, and may have some
reference to conjuring tricks.
[11] P iii, p. 267.

of processions out of doors—

> . . . running one after another about the churchyard like the prior of Pricklingham and his convent.[1]

Two other examples—

> . . . here is the door, and there is the way, farewell, gentle Geffrey.[2]

> . . . as the porters cry in Sturbridge fair, A new master, a new, and hang up the old. . . .[3]

Such phrases, probably derived from popular witticisms, interludes,[4] ballads, vulgar and obscene jokes, and the like, of which no trace now remains, show how closely Becon kept in touch with the ordinary man of his day, and help to explain the ready appeal of his works.

II

Like many of his contemporaries, Becon tried his hand at writing religious verse, but he seems to have realized that his poems were "without eloquence, rude and barbarous to behold",[5] and desisted from this form of composition after his return from exile. Some commendatory lines prefixed to John Studley's translation of Seneca's *Agamemnon* and *Medea* are signed "T.B." and have generally been attributed to Becon, but they have only to be compared with, say, the address "to the godly reader" in *The Governance of Virtue*,[6] for it to be abundantly evident that they are not his.[7]

After the fashion of the time Becon also wrote Latin verse, and some commendatory lines composed for William Turner's *Triacle* have survived.[8]

---

[1] P iii, p. 281.
[2] P iii, p. 534.
[3] ibid.
[4] " Hickscorner", to whom Becon makes several references (P iii, pp. 259, 279, 361) was a character in an allegorical interlude of the same title by Wynkyn de Worde, and denoted a travelled libertine who scoffs at religion.
[5] P ii, p. 3.
[6] See P i, p. 395.
[7] See E. M. Spearing's edition of Studley's Seneca's *Agamemnon* and *Medea*, Louvain, 1913, p. 16 f.
[8] These lines are not printed in either the folio or the Parker Society editions of Becon's works, and can only be seen in Turner's book.

CHAPTER XI

THE MAN AND HIS FAMILY

I

BECON'S contemporaries are warm in their praises of his learning, industry, and influence as a writer,[1] but of the man himself, his character and manner, they say nothing; two portraits, however, give us some idea of his appearance. His works reflect an earnest and severe piety, tempered by a strong but somewhat rudimentary sense of humour, and an enthusiastic, perhaps impulsive, temperament ; and something has already been said of the impression created by the part he took in ecclesiastical affairs. Of personal traits, however, we can glean little, apart from something of a distaste for music.[2]

Several times he mentions serious indispositions, and the portrait of 1560 is that of a sick man.[3] He was probably not constitutionally strong, and may have suffered from long periods of ill health, due perhaps to some disease which was responsible for his comparatively early death ; the motto, *vive memor lethi*, suggests that he may himself have been aware of his delicate condition. Though at times hindered or incapacitated by illness, his great output bears testimony to an unflagging application to the work to which he believed he had been called ; always he seems to have kept before him as a guiding principle the Lord's words : " Occupy till I come".[4]

[1] See the commendatory verses by Parkhurst, Calfhill, and Bomelius, P i, p. 33.
[2] *The Jewel of Joy*, P ii, pp. 429 and 430.
[3] It will be recalled that in *The Book of Matrimony*, written at that time, he refers to a long illness ; see above, p. 103.
[4] See, e.g., P i, p. 1.

II

Becon probably married very soon after the legalization of clerical marriage in 1549, but no register entry can be found to confirm this, and he tells us nothing himself ; we do not even know the name of his wife.[1]

He twice mentions his children. The *New Catechism* is dedicated to Theodore, Basil, and Rachel, and in the preface he refers to Theodore and Christophile, " which now rest in glory with our head Christ",[2] while in *The Sick Man's Salve*[3] he alludes to his son Theodore and his daughter Rachel.[4] The age of the *Son* in the *New Catechism* (" not six years old ") is probably that of Theodore, Becon's eldest surviving child, who was born in 1555.[5] About the other boy, Basil, there is some confusion. A Basil was baptized on 14th January, 1558-9, as we have seen,[6] but the age of the Basil Beacon who was admitted at King's College, Cambridge, on 27th August, 1579, is given as seventeen,[7] making his birth-date 1562. The probable explanation is that the Basil baptized in St. Stephen's, Walbrook, died, and another boy, born three years later, was given his name.

It seems, then, that Theodore I and Christophile were born before the summer of 1553, and that the former died immedi-

---

[1] Boyd's Marriage Index, in the possession of the Society of Genealogists, contains no reference to Thomas Becon. A marriage took place, however, in the church of St. Mildred Poultry on 12th January, 1548-9, between " Thomas Bacon and Cisly Wherey". The register, now preserved in St. Margaret's Lothbury, clearly shows the name as " Bacon " ; the entry, however, is only a copy made late in 1598 and certified by the parson and churchwardens on 23rd April, 1599 [I am indebted for this information to the Bishop of Stepney]. It is just possible, therefore, that an error occurred in transcription, and that the original entry actually related to Becon. On the other hand, Knox (see above, p. 78) and le Neve (see above, p. 92) spell the name " Bacon "— but the London church registers of the period contain other entries for Bacon and Beacon, so that this particular one may be of no significance.

[2] P ii, p. 5.

[3] Probably the revised edition of 1561, see above, p. 67.

[4] P iii, p. 93.

[5] P ii, p. 8 ; Theodore matriculated from St. John's College, Cambridge, 1567, aet. 12, see Venn, *Alumni*, I, i, p. 114.

[6] See above, p. 91.

[7] Venn, *Alumni*, I, i, p. 114 ; *Eton College Register*, ed. W. Sterry, No. 1698, p. 144.

ately before the family's departure for the Continent, or soon after their arrival. His name was given to the next child, born at Marburg in 1555 ; Christophile probably died there in 1556 or 1557, and Rachel may have been born sometime between 1556 and 1558 (unless she, too, saw the light in England before Becon's exile). Basil I was born very early in January, 1558-9, and died soon after ; Basil II was born in 1562.

Of Becon's surviving children, Theodore matriculated from St. John's College, Cambridge, as a pensioner in 1567 at the age of twelve. He is described as " of Norfolk". He became B.A. in 1576-7, M.A. in 1580, and M.D. in 1586. He was elected to a fellowship of his College in 1579, but soon after migrated to Oxford, where he was incorporated M.A. on 11th July, 1581, and M.D. in 1587. In the latter year he married Dorcas Smythe in St. Michael's, Cornhill ; only one child of the marriage can be traced—Elizabeth, who died at Canterbury and was buried in the Cathedral on 3rd February, 1628-9. At the time of her death she was resident in the parish of St. Alphage, Canterbury. Dr. Becon was ordained, and was Rector of Toppesfield, Essex, in 1603-4 ; this seems to have been his only preferment, and he appears to have lived for the latter part of his life in Canterbury, possibly engaged in a medical practice. He died there, and was buried in the Cathedral on 21st March, 1619-20.[1]

Basil II went to Eton as a King's Scholar in 1574 and passed from there to King's College, Cambridge, where he was admitted scholar on 27th August, 1579. He graduated B.A. in 1583-4 and M.A. in 1587, and was fellow of his College, 1582-1587. Ordained, like his brother, he held the following preferments : Warehorn, Kent, 1587-1608 ;[2] Snave, Kent, 1597 ; Hawkinge, 1597-99 ; Herne Hill, 1605 ; Waltham, 1610-1639. He is also said to have been Vicar of Silkstone in Yorkshire. On 2nd October, 1588, in St. Michael's, Cornhill, he married Anne Coale, and by her had five children, entered in the baptism register at Warehorn : Elizabeth, Rachel,

---

[1] Venn, *Alumni*, I, i, p. 114 ; Foster, *Alumni Oxonienses*, i, p. 94b ; *Registers* of St. Michael's, Cornhill, and Canterbury Cathedral, Harl. Society.
[2] Venn, *Alumni*, simply has 1587, but the Registers are signed " Basil Becon, Parson", up to 1608. No doubt he held Warehorn in plurality with other livings.

Thomas, Theodore, and John who died within a few weeks of birth ; others may have been born and baptized elsewhere.[1]

Rachel married William Beswick or Berwick, a gentleman of Kent, and died without issue.[2]

In the preface to the *New Catechism* Becon tells his children how from their very cradles he had tried to bring them up in the ways of true religion,[3] and one wonders whether he followed the method described in that work :

> So soon as the children be able to speak plainly, let them even from their cradles be taught to utter not vain, foolish, and wanton, but grave, sober, and godly words ; as God, Jesus Christ, faith, love, hope, patience, goodness, peace, &c. And when they be able to pronounce whole sentences, let the parents teach their children such sentences as may kindle in them a love toward virtue, and an hatred against vice and sin ; as for an ensample : God alone saveth me. Christ by his death hath redeemed me. The Holy Ghost sanctifieth me. . . .[4]

He certainly expresses the greatest satisfaction at their progress,[5] and we cannot doubt that Theodore, Rachel, and Basil fulfilled the early promise of which their father was justly proud.

[1] See Venn, *Alumni*, I, i, p. 114; W. Sterry, *op. cit.*, No. 1698, p. 144 ; *Registers* of St. Michael's, Cornhill (Harl. Socy.), and Warehorn parish registers.
[2] *Visitation of Kent*, 1592, Harl. lxxv ; *Visitation of Kent*, 1619, Harl. xlii. In the former Rachel is described as " d. of Thomas Beacon gent one of the Prebendares of Christes Churche in Canterburye".
[3] P ii, p. 6.
[4] P ii, p. 348.
[5] P ii, p. 6.

K

DETACHED NOTE A

BIOGRAPHICAL MATERIAL

1. BECON'S OWN WRITINGS

CERTAIN works (Bib. I A, nos. 3, 4, 6, 13, 23, 29 and 34) are in dialogue form, and one of the interlocutors, *Philemon*, generally represents Becon. From the statements and allusions of this character information can be gathered concerning his family, life, and circumstances. In *The Jewel of Joy* certain references to Cambridge are put into the mouth of another character, *Christopher*. Many of the prefaces to the works reveal important facts about Becon's life, and sometimes the dedications are suggestive. His second recantation is also valuable. But when everything has been extracted from his works, there are many large and important gaps to fill; his silences are sometimes significant, but more often perplexing.

2. CONTEMPORARY DOCUMENTS AND SOURCES

There are incidental references to Becon in Bradford's *Works* (PS), Bale's *Catalogus*, Brett's *Narrative*, Foxe, the *Letters and Papers* for Henry VIII's reign, Machyn's *Diary*, Parker's *Correspondence* (PS) and *Episcopal Register*, the *Registers* of St. Stephen's Walbrook, the Visitation of the Norwich diocese (1532) and Wriothesley's *Chronicle*. Becon signs two letters sent from Frankfort to Calvin in 1555. Records and documents mentioning him are printed by Ames, *Typ. Ant.*, Arber, *Transcript of the Stationers' Register*, Ayre, preface to PS edition of his works, Burnet, *Reformation*, Gee, *The Elizabethan Clergy*, Dixon, HCE, Foxe, and Strype, *Parker* and *Annals*. His name is in the Frankfort *Standesliste* for 1555 (Garrett, *Exiles*), and in the *Catalogus* prefixed to the 1557 (Latin) edition of Cranmer's *Defence* (*Defensio verae et catholicae doctrinae de Sacramento*) published in Emden. Newcourt,

Repertorium, and Hennessy, *Nov. Repert.*, list details of institutions to London benefices, some of which refer to Becon.

All the material given under headings 1 and 2 has been published, but very little of it has been used by previous biographers.

3. CONTEMPORARY MATERIAL
UNPUBLISHED AND HITHERTO UNUSED

A Register of Ordinations in the diocese of Norwich, 1531-1561—a paper book in very bad condition in the Bishop's Registry at Norwich, containing entries relative to ordinations by John Underwood, titular Bishop of Chalcedon.

4. SECONDARY SOURCES OF INFORMATION

These are sufficiently indicated in the footnotes, and require no further mention here.

5. BIOGRAPHICAL NOTICES

These vary greatly in scope and value. The earliest is in Bale's *Catalogus*, which gives little precise information, apart from the fact that when it was written Becon was in Marburg ; it is biased and apologetic in tone. Next comes Lupton's short and inaccurate account in *The History of the Moderne Protestant Divines* (1637). Tanner's notice (1747) is based upon Bale, but has a few extra biographical details, including the statement that Becon was Vicar of Brenzett, an error, the source of which cannot be discovered. The accounts in Ritson's *Bibliographia Poetica* (1802), Brook's *Lives of the Puritans* (1813), Chalmers' *General Bibliographical Dictionary* (1812-1813), and Granger's *Biographical History of England* (1824), and other similar works, are meagre and of no consequence. The prefaces to selections of Becon's works published by the R.T.S. (*British Reformers*, 1828-1831)—reviewed by Dr. Alexander in the American *Princeton Review*—and by S.P.C.K. (1836) contain nothing of additional interest, and simply reproduce the facts (and errors) accumulated by previous writers.

The first serious attempt to write Becon's life is to be found in the biographical notice by the Rev. John Ayre prefixed to the first volume of the PS edition of Becon's works. This, while not entirely free from the errors of its predecessors, makes use of hitherto neglected material, including Foxe, Strype, and Becon's own works, to which earlier biographers unaccountably neglect to refer. Ayre's account has proved invaluable to all subsequent writers, though he is somewhat too laudatory and partial—understandable faults, when the circumstances at the time of its composition, and the objects of the Parker Society, are taken into account. This notice appeared in 1843, and full-length articles based upon it are included in Cooper, *Athenae* (1858), and in the DNB (1885 ff.). The shorter notice in the Census in Miss Garrett's *Exiles* is valuable for its references to Becon's life on the Continent during Mary's reign.

DETACHED NOTE B

THE DATE OF THOMAS BECON'S BIRTH

THE data for determining when Becon was born are meagre and inconsistent. One portrait is inscribed " AETATIS SVAE. 41 AN°. DNI. 1553 " and the other, " ANNO AETATIS SVAE. 49. 1560", but calculation will show that these figures do not give one consistent birth-date agreeable to all the ages and years stated. They only show that he must have been born between 25th March, 1512, and 24th March, 1513-1514.

Turning now to Becon's graduation, we find that he was admitted B.A. in 1530-31. This would normally be after four years study. His *stans in quadragesima* probably began on Ash Wednesday, 22nd February, 1530-1, and ended in the following April. This would mean that he entered the University not later than March, 1526-7, and since the freshman of those days was usually fourteen or fifteen years old, it would give us a birth-date not earlier than January, 1511-12, nor later than the end of 1512-13.

While it is clear from the data that we cannot fix Becon's birth-date with any precision, I am inclined to think that it will not be much wide of the mark to place it between 25th March, 1512, and 24th March, 1512-13, that is, in 1512, old style.

DETACHED NOTE C

BECON'S ACADEMICAL CAREER

THOMAS BECON proceeded B.A. in 1530-1, and there is no doubt that this was his only academical distinction. The certificate which he completed in 1561 is conclusive ; on it he describes himself simply as " Baccalaur.Art.". Occasionally he is designated S.T.B.[1] or S.T.P.[2], but he is always referred to as " Mr. Becon".

Biographers, however, have showered honours upon him. Tanner says :

> . . . in academia Cantabrig. studiis philosophicis et theologicis imbutus per varios academicorum honorum gradus ad cathedram theologicam ascendit.[3]

and Bale describes him as " artium magister".[4] Ayre states that he " graduated doctor of divinity " at Cambridge,[5] and the DNB also designates him D.D., while Venn says that he is reputed to have been B.D.[6] It is also asserted by Lupton that " in the reigne of King Edward the sixth, he did professe Divinity in the flourishing University of Oxford",[7] and Holland calls him " Professor of Theology " at Oxford, *temp.* Edward VI,[8] while Cooper states that " he appears, but at what period is unknown, to have commenced D.D. at Oxford".[9]

---

[1] Hennessy, *Nov. Repert.*, p. 80 ; Parker's *Register*, p. 802.

[2] Portraits ; Newcourt, *Repertorium*, i, p. 330 ; Parker's *Register*, pp. 204-205, 833, 834. Apart from Tanner's remarks (see next n.), it may have been this title, wrongly interpreted, which has given rise to the idea that Becon was a university professor.

[3] p. 85.

[4] *Index*, p. 430.

[5] P i, p. vii.

[6] *Alumni*, I, i, p. 114.

[7] *op. cit.*, p. 331.

[8] *Heroologia*, p. 179.

[9] *Athenae*, i, p. 247.

For none of these statements is there the least foundation. As for Becon's association with Oxford, his name does not appear either in Bliss's *Athenae Oxonienses*[1] or in Wood's *Fasti Oxonienses*. Probably there has been some confusion between Thomas and his son Theodore, who graduated M.D. at Cambridge in 1586 and was incorporated M.D. at Oxford in 1587.

DETACHED NOTE D

BECON'S ORDINATION AND FIRST PREFERMENT

THERE is no doubt that Becon was ordained exorcist and acolyte on 25th May, 1532, sub-deacon on 13th March, 1532-3, deacon on 29th March, 1533, and priest on 12th April, 1533. The purpose of this note is simply to consider the discrepancy between these facts and Becon's statement, in the preface to the folio edition, that at the time of writing he had travailed twenty-six years in the ministry. His supposed preferment to the vicarage of Brenzett is also discussed.

I

1. From what date is the period of 26 years to be calculated ?

(i) The preface is dated 17th January, 1564 (i.e., 1563-4, for the last volume of the folio edition appeared during 1564). Twenty-six years deducted from this gives a commencement date for Becon's ministry of January, 1537-8.

(ii) But the dedication of the folio edition is to the Archbishops and Bishops of the English Church, and their names appear at the head of the preface, which is partly addressed to them. If dedication and preface were composed at the same time, they must have been written between the consecration of Cheney as Bishop of Gloucester and Bristol on 19th April, 1562, and the death of Kitchin of Llandaff on

---

[1] Apart from a reference to Dr. Richard Smith's attack upon him, see above, pp 98-99.

31st October, 1563, since both prelates are mentioned, and the rest were either consecrated or translated before, or died or were translated after, these two dates. This gives a commencement date for Becon's ministry somewhere between April, 1536, and October, 1537.

(iii) If the preface was written first, before the first volume of the folio edition went to press in 1560, and the dedication and date were added afterwards, when the whole work was issued, a commencement date for his ministry of 1534 would be obtained.

Of these possibilities (ii) is the most likely and (iii) the least likely. Even so, 3-4 years must be accounted for.

2. What did Becon mean by " ministry " ? There are four possible interpretations :

(a) The period subsequent to his ordination as acolyte and exorcist on 25th May, 1532.

(b) The period subsequent to his ordination as priest on 12th April, 1533.

(c) The period during which, by preaching or otherwise, he professed protestant opinions and exercised a "reformed" ministry.

(d) The period during which he exercised an active or full-time ministry, as opposed to teaching.

By adopting one or other of these suggestions in conjunction with the various possibilities set out in (1) above, several approximate solutions to the problem can be obtained, but none is satisfactory.

Bearing in mind the uncertainty of the data, and Becon's habitual inaccuracy in mentioning dates and periods of time, we may assume that in computing the 26 years he omitted the time he spent in teaching. This at any rate gives the nearest result.

II

Tanner seems to have been the first to state that soon after ordination Becon became Vicar of Brenzett, near New Romney, in Kent.   Cranmer's *Register*, however, shows that this is entirely unfounded ; the institutions to the church of St. Eanswith are as follows:

26th Sept., 1535. Wm. Morfoyle, A.M., on the death of Thomas Daykyn.

8th July, 1538. Henry Becher, S.T.P., on the death of the last incumbent (unnamed).

28th July, 1541. Thomas Chapman, on the death of the last incumbent (unnamed).

Nor did Becon later hold this living, as Parker's Register shows :

12th Dec., 1562. John Pady, on the death of Tho. Chapman.

14th July, 1567. John Whytynge, on the resignation of John Pady.

How then did Becon's name become connected with Brenzett ?

1. Brenzett may be a mistake for another place of like sound or spelling, with which Tanner discovered that Becon had some association of which we now know nothing. Great Bricet, the parish next to Nettlestead, the seat of Becon's patron, Lord Wentworth, was an attractive guess, but nothing could be traced.

2. Tanner may have had evidence, which has not been preserved, that Becon actually had some connexion with Brenzett, either during his Kentish retirement, or as Canon of Canterbury.

3. Most probably, however, there has been confusion between Thomas Becon and his son Basil II, who in 1597 was rector of the parish of Snave, which adjoins Brenzett. In 1917 the two parishes were united, but it seems that in earlier days the Rectors of Snave occasionally served Brenzett in the absence of a Vicar of the latter. Behind the legend of Becon's connexion with Brenzett may well lie some recollection of his son's association with the parish while at Snave.

DETACHED NOTE E

A SELECT COLLATION OF THE 1542 AND FOLIO EDITIONS OF THE *POTATION FOR LENT*

THE references are to the PS edition of the folio revision of the *Potation* ; 91/41 denotes page 91 of vol. i, line 41.

	Folio	1542
91/41	. . . the doctrine of penance (as they term it) . . .	ye mooste confortable Sacrament of Penāce . . .
91/42	taught unto penitent sinners . . .	exercised toward penitent sinners . . .
91/48	. . . the most blessed sacrament of Christ's very body and blood . . .	. . . of the Altare Christes very body and bloud . . .
91/51	this time of Lent	this holy time of Lent . . .
	and at all other times also . . .	" and . . . also " omitted.
94/39	. . . penance . . .	. . . this Sacrament of penāce . . .
110/24	OF CERTAIN CEREMONIES HERETOFORE USED IN THE CHURCH AT THE TIME OF LENT . . .	of the Ceremonies used in the churche this tyme of Lent . . .
110/27	. . . was . . .	. . . is . . . (and so throughout).
117/8 /13 /15	. . . sacrament of Christ's body and blood . . .	. . . Sacrament of the Altare . . .
117/26	. . . the holy mysteries of Christ's body and blood . . .	. . . the body of oure LORDE . . .
119/8	. . . the holy mysteries of Christ's body and blood . . .	. . . ye very body of Christ . . .
119/16	. . . the sacrament . . .	. . . Christes body . . .
119/21	. . . sacrament of the body and blood of Christ . . .	. . . Sacrament of the Altare . . .

[*Continued overleaf*

	Folio	1542
119/24		[after " sacrament "] : Christes very body & bloude . . .
119/45	. . . with the body . . .	. . . with the true body . . .
120/2	. . . RECEIVED THE SAC- RAMENT . . .	. . . received the mooste blessed Sacramēt of the Altare . . .
120/3 /4	. . . received the sacrament of the body and blood of our Lord Jesus Christ . . .	. . . received the body of our LORDE Jesus Christ, and wᵗ that same mooste glorious bodye tasted also his most precious bloud . . .
120/17		[after " King "] : where no terrestrial & cor- ruptible meate is eaten, but euen the very bodye of ye pure & immaculate Lambe Jesus Christ . . .
120/36 /37	. . . the holy mysteries of the body and blood of our Lord and alone Saviour Jesu Christ . . .	the very body of our Lord Jesus Christ . . .
121/44	. . . penance . . .	. . . the holy Sacrament of Penaunce . . .
121/45	. . . Christ's body and blood . . .	. . . [sacrament] of the Altare . . .

DETACHED NOTE F

BECON'S *CATECHISM*

THE catechism was properly a simple and succint method
of instruction by question and answer, and the Reformation produced admirable examples in Luther's *Short
Catechism* and the Catechism in the Edwardine Prayer Books.
Becon's metrical Catechism seems to have been similar in
scope, and the *Demands of Holy Scripture* conforms closely to
the simple catechetical form, but his *New Catechism* is a work

of wholly different character. It is actually a comprehensive system of doctrine thrown into catechism form, and is probably the most extensive composition of its kind ever produced by an Anglican theologian—larger even than Hammond's *Practical Catechism*. Like other longer works in catechetical form, it is no doubt indebted to Luther's *Greater Catechism*, in which the question and answer method is abandoned in favour of an extended expository treatment.

Dr. Jacobs, however, has shown that Becon's *New Catechism* is beholden to Luther for more than its form alone. It is, he says,

> . . . an independent development by one in whose mind and heart, Luther's explanations, often in their very words, are deeply fixed, and who with great freedom, expands and develops what he has drawn from this source and thoroughly assimilated.[1]

Only in the section on the Lord's Supper does Dr. Jacobs note an almost entire absence of Lutheran influence ; there, he considers, " the traces of the Calvinistic movement . . . are very apparent", though we have observed a more pronouncedly Zwinglian or Cranmerian tendency.

This dependence upon Luther's explanations leads Dr. Jacobs to suggest that Becon may well have been wholly or partly responsible for the preparation of Cranmer's *Catechism* of 1548. He considers that this was probably made from the Nürnberg Catechism of 1533, under the Primate's supervision, by one of his chaplains—either Taylor, Ponet, or Becon, and he regards the latter as most likely to have performed or assisted in the work.[2]

---

[1] *op. cit.*, p. 325. For examples of Lutheran influence, see Jacobs's article, " The Lutheran Element in Early English Catechisms " in *The Lutheran Church Review*, No. 3, July, 1888, pp. 173-177.

[2] See *op. cit.*, pp. 314-325 for a full discussion.

GENEALOGICAL TABLE 1

THOMAS BECON'S FAMILY

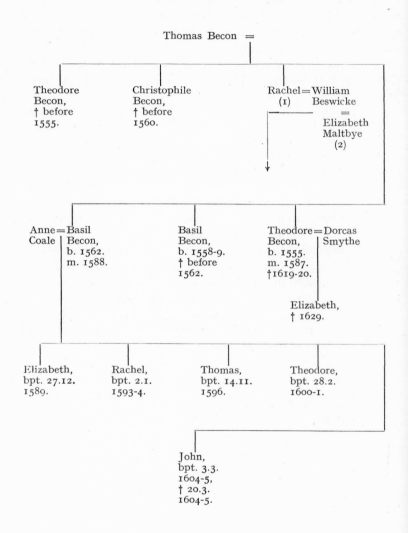

Thomas Becon =

Theodore
Becon,
† before
1555.

Christophile
Becon,
† before
1560.

Rachel=William
(1)   Beswicke
          =
          Elizabeth
          Maltbye
          (2)

Anne=Basil
Coale │ Becon,
        b. 1562.
        m. 1588.

Basil
Becon,
b. 1558-9.
† before
1562.

Theodore=Dorcas
Becon,   │ Smythe
b. 1555.
m. 1587.
†1619-20.

Elizabeth,
† 1629.

Elizabeth,
bpt. 27.12.
1589.

Rachel,
bpt. 2.1.
1593-4.

Thomas,
bpt. 14.11.
1596.

Theodore,
bpt. 28.2.
1600-1.

John,
bpt. 3.3.
1604-5,
† 20.3.
1604-5.

GENEALOGICAL TABLE 2

INTER-RELATIONSHIPS OF DEDICATEES
OF BECON'S WORKS

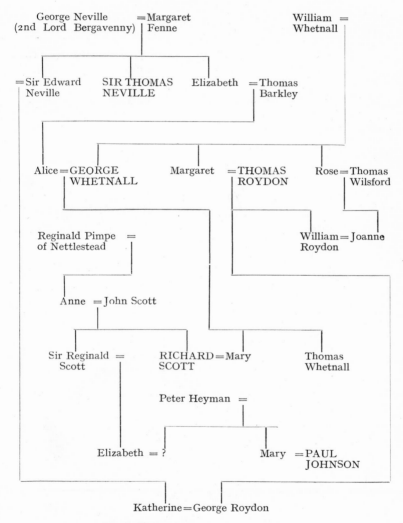

The dedicatees' names are in CAPITALS.

BIBLIOGRAPHIES

I

THOMAS BECON'S WORKS

A. GENUINE WORKS

THESE have been listed chronologically according to the composition date, or where that cannot be accurately ascertained, the publication date. Where neither is certainly known, the work has been located as nearly as possible.

* date of composition unknown.

† dates of composition and publication unknown.

§ published work not included in the folio edition.

¶ work no longer extant.

§ ¶ 1. First recantation, February or March, 1540-1. Fragments included in the second recantation, No. 15

2. Newes out of heauen, by Theodore Basille. Probably composed for Christmas, 1541. *John Mayler for John Gough* : London [1541-2 ?]. 8vo. [*STC* 1739].

 2a. another edition. *John Mayler for John Gough* : London, 1542. 8vo. [*STC* 1740].

3. A Christmas Bankette garnyshed with many pleasaunt and deynty dishes, by Theodore Basille. Composed for Christmas, 1541. *John Mayler for John Gough* : London, 1542. 8vo. [*STC* 1713].

 3a. another edition. *John Mayler for John Gough* : London, 1542. 8vo. [*STC* 1714].

 3b. Een Christlick Werschap, oft Een Kersmis Bancket. Einen veghelicken Christen mensche seer nut ende profijtelick, te lesen. . . . Ouerghesettet wt het Engelsch in gueden Duytsche, etc. [*Campen*], 1543. 8vo.

4. A potation or drinkynge for this holi time of Lent. Composed in February or March, 1541-2. *John Mayler for John Gough* : London, 1542. 8vo. [*STC* 1749].

 4a. another edition. A Potaciõ or drīkynge for this holy tyme of Lēt very cõfortable for al penitēt sinners w̄ a table in the end, newly prepared & diligētly ouersene by Theodor Basille. *Iohñ Meyler for Iohñ Gough* : London, 1543. 8vo. [*STC* 1750].

* 5. A newe patheway vnto praier, by T. Basille. *John Mayler for John Gough* : London, 1542. 8vo. [*STC* 1734].

 5a. another edition. The right pathwaye unto Prayer, ful of muche godly fruyte and Christen knowledge, wyth a Table in the end, lately made and newly recognised by Theodore Basille. *Iohñ Mayler for Iohñ Gough* : London, 1543. 8vo. [*STC* 1756].

6. A pleasaunt newe Nosegaye, full of many godly and swete floures, lately gathered by Theodore Basille. Composed in May, 1542. *Iohñ Maylerre for Iohñ Gough* : *London*, 1542. 8vo. [*STC* 1742].

6a. another edition—as before, 1543.

7. The new pollecy of warre, wherin is declared not only how yᵗ mooste cruell Tyraunt the great Turke maye be ouercome, but also all other enemies of the Christen publique weale, lately diuised by Theodore Basille. [with woodcuts]. Composed August or September, 1542. *Iohñ Maylerre for Iohñ Gough* : *London*, 1542. 8vo. [*STC* 1735].

7a. another edition with new title : The true defence of peace [fragment only]. *John Mayler for John Gough* : *London*, 1542. [*STC* 1775].

7b. another edition. The true defēce of Peace, wherin is declaredde the cause of all warres now a days, and how they maye be pacified, called before the Pollecye of Warre, devysed & lately recognised by Theodore Basille. [with woodcuts]. *Iohñ Mayler for Iohñ Gough* : *London*, 1543. 8vo. [*STC* 1776].

7c. another edition—as before, 1544. [Ames, *Typ.Ant.*, iii, p. 543].

* 8. A devout and godly prayer, for all degrees and estates, made upon the hundred and fifteenth Psalm. . . . This was appended to No. 7b, but was afterwards subjoined to No. 9, in the folio edition.

* 9. Davids harpe ful of armony, by Theodore Basille. *John Mayler for John Gough* : *London*, 1542. 8vo. [*STC* 1717].

* 10. Preface to Coverdale's translation of Bullinger's *Der Christlich Eestand* (*Tig.* 1540, 12mo.), entitled The golden boke of christen matrimonye. *John Mayler for John Gough* : *London*, 1542. 8vo. This translation, says Becon, was " for the more ready sale, set forth in my name by the hungry printer with my preface . . ." P i, p. 29. [*STC* 1723].

10a. another edition, as before, 1543. [*STC* 1724].

10b. another edition, The christen state of matrimony, moost necessary & profitable for all thē, that entend to liue quietly and godlye in the christē state of holy wedlock, newly set forth in Englysh—as before, 1546.

† § ¶ 11. Catechism in verse : nothing is known of this work, which Becon replaced by A New Catechism in the folio edition, retaining only the prefatory verses (see P i, p. 29 ; also Bale, *Index*, fol. 175b : Poole and Bateson, pp. 430-431).

† § ¶ 12. Christmas Carrols very new and godly. This work is not extant, but is mentioned in the proclamation of prohibited books, 8th July, 1546—see *L. & P.* Henry VIII, xxi, i, p. 611, No. 1233; also Foxe, v, p. 567.

13. A new yeares gyfte more precious than golde, worthy to be embrased no lesse ioyfully than thākfully of every true christē man, *etc.* Composed in December, 1542. *Iohñ Mayler for Iohñ Gough* : *London*, 1543. 8vo. [*STC* 1738].

* 14. An inuectyue agenst swearing, by Theodore Basille. *J. Mayler for J. Gough* : *London*, 1543. 8vo. [*STC* 1731].

14a. another edition, as before, 8vo. No date. [*STC* 1732].

§ 15. Second recantation, 8th July, 1543—see Foxe, v, App. XII.

16. The Governance of Virtue ; probably composed late in 1543, and first published (anonymously ?) before 1547.

16a. The gouernance of vertue, *London* [1549]—or 1550.   16mo. [*STC* 1725].

16b. another edition. *J. Day* : *London* [? 1560]. 16mo. [*STC* 1726].

16c. another edition.   The Gouernaunce of Vertur, teaching all faythful christiãs how they oughte daily to leade their lyfe, & fruitfully to spend their time vnto the glorye of God & the health of their owne soules.   Newlye corrected and augmēted.   [with a portrait].   *Iohn Day* : *London*, 1566, 8vo. [*STC* 1727].

16d. another edition. *J. Day* : *London*, 1578. 16mo. [*STC* 1728].

16e. another edition. *Simon Stafford* : *London*, 1607. 12mo.

17. An Invective agaynst whoredom and al other abominations of uncleanesse, a worke most necessary for thys present time.   In english verse. [folio ed. title]. Composed between 1543 and 1546 ?   Published 1548 ?

18. A dialogue of Christ's Nativity between the Angel and the Shepherds.   Composed between 1543 and 1546 ?   Published 1548 ?— see P ii, p. 427.

[18a. This work was probably revised before inclusion in the folio edition, where it is entitled, A new Dialoge betwene the Angel of God and the Shepherds of yͤ felde, concerning the natiuity & byrth of Jesus Christ our Lord and Savior, no lesse godly than swete and pleasaunte to reade. In english verse.]

¶ 19. The Shield of Salvation—a translation from the Latin made during Becon's sojourn in the Midlands, but apparently never published and not now extant ; see *Works*, P ii, p. 427.   Probable date 1545-1546 ?

¶ 20. The Commemoration of Death—another work translated from the Latin between 1543 and 1546, but not published and not extant under this title.   It may, however, be the work entitled The Praise of Death, see No. 66, also P ii, p. 427.

21. The Solace of the soule veri comfortable against the bytter stormes of sicknes and death greatly encouragyng the faithful both patiently and thankfully to suffer the good pleasure of God in all kinde of aduersytye. [folio ed. title]. *W. Hill*, 1548. [*STC* 1774]. A translation from the Latin, see P ii, p. 427.

22. An homely against whoredom.   Composed early in 1547. Published in the first Book of Homilies, July, 1547.

23. The Jewel of Joy.   Probably composed 1547-1548.   The earliest copy extant (8vo. *John Day* : *London*, 1553) is without pagination : sigs. B-Y each in eight leaves, Aa in four leaves ; title-page, all before sig. B, and a small portion of sig. Aa i, are wanting.   " It is not unlikely that, owing to the accession of Queen Mary, the printing of the book was never completed."—Brit. Mus. Cat. It is improbable, however, that this imperfect copy was the first.

* § 24. The Physycke of the soule, wherein thou shalt finde many Godly emplastures & confortable salues agaynst al spiritual diseases, very necessary to be red of the true christens in these last and perilous days.   Set forth by Thomas Becon. Sold by *W. Hill*. 10th July, 1549. 16mo. 24 pp. [*STC* 1741].

§ 25. A humble peticyon to the lord, practysed in the commune prayer of the whole famylye at Shene, during the trouble of the . . .duke of Somerset . . . gathered & set furth by T. Becon, minister there. Which trouble began the VI of October the year of our Lord MD.XLIX and ended the VI of Febuarye then next ensuing. [This is appended to The spyrytual and precious pearle, probably

C

Coverdale's translation of a work by Otho Wermylierus, with a prefatory epistle by Edward Duke of Somerset—see bibliography attached to Cooper's notice of Coverdale, No. 25, *Athenae*, i, p. 273] *London*, 1550. 12mo.

26. The floure of godlye prayers most worthy to be vsed in these our dayes, for the sauegarde, healthe, and comforte of al degres and estates, *etc. Iohn Day*: *London*, 1551. 8vo. [*STC* 1720]. Probably composed in 1550.

26a. Selections from Becon's Flower of Godly Prayers, etc., pub. in The Book of Private Devotions ; containing a collection of the most valuable early devotions of the Reformers and their successors, in the English Church. . . ., ed. the Rev. E. Bickersteth, *London*, 1839. 8vo.

* 27. The Principles of Christen Religion necessary to be knowen of the faythfull. . . . *J. Daye* : *London* [? 1550]. 8vo. [*STC* 1751].

27a. another edition—as above [? 1552]. [*STC* 1752].

27b. another edition—as above, 1569. [*STC* 1753].

* 28. The Castell of Comforte, in the whiche it is euidently proued, y* God alone absolueth, and freli forgeueth the sinnes of so many as vnfaynedly repent and turne vnto hym, *etc. Ihon Daye & William Seres* : *London* [? 1550]. 16mo. [*STC* 1712].

* 29. The Fortresse of the faythfull agaynst ye cruel assautes of pouertie and honger newlye made for the comforte of poore nedye Christians. *Iohn Daye & William Seres* : *London*, 1550. 8vo. [*STC* 1721].

* § 30. Latin poem appended to A Preseruatiue, or Triacle, agaynst the poyson of Pelagius, by Wm. Turner. [*R. Jugge*] *for A. Hester*, 1551. 8vo. [*STC* 24368].

* 31. A fruitful treatise of fasting. . . . *J. Day* : *London* [? 1552]. [Folio ed. title : A fruitfull treatise of fasting, wherin is declared what ye Christen fast is, how we ought to fast, & what the true use of fasting is]. [*STC* 1722].

31a. ? another edition—A treatise of fasting, by T.B.—see Ames. *Typ.Ant.*, iv, p. 156.

† 32. The Christian Knight. [folio ed. title : The Christen knighte teaching the Warriers of God not onely how they must preuaile against Satan and his wicked army in this worlde, but also how they may liue before God with a quiet and mery conscience].

† 33. The Pomaunder of prayer. Composed before 1553. Publication date of the first ed. unknown.

33a. The Pomāder of Prayer. Wherein is contained many godly Prayers, whereunto are added certayne Meditations called S. Augustines, which, beyng redde with a feruent mynde, wyll profyt much, and stur thee to vertue (The xv Ooes. The Letanie). *London*, 1558. 8vo. [*STC* 1744].

33b. another edition, with portrait. *Iohn Daye* : *Lōdon* [? 1560]. 8vo. [*STC* 1745].

33c. another edition, with portrait. As 33b, 1561. [*STC* 1746].

33d. another edition, *John Daye* : *London*, 1565. 8vo. [*STC* 1747].

33e. another edition, The Pommander of Prayers. *J. Daye* : *London*, 1578. 8vo. [*STC* 1748].

33f. another edition, in Bickersteth's Book of Private Devotions, see 26a.

L

† 34. The Sick Man's Salve. Composed before 1553 ; it cannot be ascertained whether the ed. of 1561 is the first or not. [folio ed. title : The Sycke Mans Salue, wherin the faithfull Christians may learne both how to behaue themselves paciently and thankefully in the tyme of syckness and also vertuously to dispose their temporall goodes and finally to prepare themselves gladly and godly to dye].

 34a. The Sycke Mans Salue. Wherin the faithfull christians may learne both how to behaue them selues paciently and thankefully, in the tyme of sickenes, *etc.* [portrait]. [*J. Day : London*], 1561. 8vo. [*STC* 1757].

 34b. another edition. *Ihon Day : London*, 1565. 8vo.

 34c. another edition. *J. Day : London*, 1568. [*STC* 1758].

 34d. another edition. *J. Day : London*, 1570. 8vo. [*STC* 1759].

 34e. another edition. *J. Daye : London*, 1572. 8vo. [*STC* 1760].

 34f. another edition. *Iohn Daye : London*, 1574. 8vo. [*STC* 1761].

 34g. another edition. 1577. [*STC* 1762].

 34h. another edition. [? *London*, ? 1580].

 34i. another edition. *Thomas Vautroullier : Edinburgh*, 1584. 8vo. [*STC* 1763].

 34j. another edition. *Printed by the Assignes of Richard Daye : London*, 1585. 8vo. [*STC* 1764].

 34k. another edition. *Printed by P. Short for the Assignes of R. Day : London*, 1594. 8vo. [*STC* 1765].

 34l. another edition. Salue for a sicke man. *Cambridge*, 1595. 8vo. [*STC* 1766].

 34m. another edition. *Printed for the Company of the Stationers : London*, 1601. 8vo. [*STC* 1767].

 34n. another edition. As 34m. 1604. 8vo. [*STC* 1768].

 34o. another edition, As 34m. 1607. 8vo. [*STC* 1769].

 34p. another edition. 1611. [*STC* 1770].

 34q. another edition. *Edbg., A. Hart*, 1613. 8vo. [*STC* 1771].

 34r. another edition. As 34m. [16(3)1]. 8vo. [*STC* 1772].

 34s. another edition. As 34m. 1632. 8vo. [*STC* 1773].

§ ¶ 35. Preparationes ad eucharistiam : incipit—" Primo notandum est, quod omnia. . . ." See Bale, *Index*, fol. 172, Poole and Bateson ed. p. 430.

§¶ 36. Bale, *Index*, fol. 172—Poole and Bateson ed. p. 430, mentions Olfactorium spirituale, with the incipit, " Legitur in tertio libro Regum". This is neither the Nosegay (No. 6) nor the Pomander (No. 33), and may be Turner's Spiritual Nosegay ascribed to Becon in error—see Foxe, v, p. 567.

37. The c. iii Psalme made in Englishe Meter, by Thomas Becon, for a thankesgeving unto God, immediately after hys deliveraunce out of prison, whose emprysonmente began the 16. day of August, the yeare of our Lord 1553, and ended the 22. of Marche, then next ensuing. First published in volume iii of the folio ed. November, 1563.

38. Psalm cxii rendered into English verse. Though undated, this appears to belong to the same time as No. 37.

* 39. A confortable Epistle, too Goddes faythfull people in Englande, wherein is declared the cause of takynge awaye the true Christen religion from them, & howe it maye be recouered and obtayned

agayne, *etc.* *At the signe of the goldē Bibel: Strasburgh.* [*H. Singleton* : *London*], 1554. 8vo. [*STC* 1716]. Preface added in folio ed. 6th October, 1563.

* 40. An humble supplicacion vnto God, for the restoringe of hys holye woorde, vnto the church of Englande. [anon.]. *Strasburg in Elsas.* [*London* : *H. Singleton*], 1544 [*sic STC* 1730 : actually 1554]. 8vo.

§ * 41. Anthologia Lactantii Firmiani elegantissimas sententias, easque tam pietate, quam doctrina illustres, complectus : recenter in locos digesta communes per Thomam Beconum. *Lugduni apud Clementem Baudinum,* 1558 ; colophon, Marburg, 1557 ; ded. to Alexander Nowell. 8vo. [A copy in the Cosin Library, Durham University].

† 42. The Displayeng of the popishe Masse : wherein thou shalt see, what a wicked Idol the Masse is, and what great difference there is betwene the Lordes Supper and the Popes Masse : Again what Popes brought in every part of the Masse, and counted it together in such monstrous sort, as it is now used in yᵉ Popes kyngdome. [folio ed. title].

[42a. Lowndes, *Bibl. Manual* i, p. 143, mentions an edition in Latin, *Basel,* 1559].

42b. another edition. *Printed by A. G.* [*Anne Griffin*], *for the Company of Stationers* : *London,* 1637. 12mo. [*STC* 1719].

§ * 43. Coenae Sacrosanctae Domini nostri, & Missae Papisticae, Comparatio, *etc.* pp. 253. *Ex Officina I. Oporini* : *Basileae,* 1559. 8vo. [see no. 56].

† § ¶ 44. Introductionem ad pietatem.

† § ¶ 45. Locorum communium sylvulam.

† § ¶ 46. Gnomothecam Salomonis.

† § ¶ 47. Sententias Iobi, David, et Tobiae.

† § ¶ 48. Miscellanea religionis.

† § ¶ 49. De authoritate verbi Dei.

† § ¶ 50. De oratione homelias aliquot.

† § ¶ 51. Iosuae Syrachi gnomologiam.

† § ¶ 52. Xenophontis flosculos.

Nos. 44-52 are listed by Bale, *Catalogus,* p. 757 ; he introduces them with the words, " In Germania Latine congessit. . . ." These works must have been published on the Continent prior to 1557, the date of the *Catalogus.* Bale's list also includes No. 41. None of these was subsequently translated into English or published in England.

53. A new Catechisme set forth Dialoge wise in famillare talke betwene the father and the son. Composed 1559-1560 and first published in the folio edition.

54. The booke of Matrimony both profitable and comfortable for all them that entende quietly and godly to lyue in the holy state of honourable wedlocke. Probably composed at the same time as No. 53 (except the preface, which is identical with No. 10, apart from a new final paragraph).

55. The Common places of the holy Scripture : containing certayne articles of Christen religion, moste necessary to be knowen of all true Christians in this Wicked and troublous time, both for yᵉ purenesse of the doctrine, and for the quietnesse of their conscience. Preface dated 10th June, 1562 ; first published in the folio edition.

56. A Comparison betwene the Lordes Supper, and the Popes Masse. A free rendering into English, with additions, and the omission of the catenae of Patristic authorities, of No. 43. First published in the folio edition.

* 57. Certayne Articles of Christen Religion, proued and confirmed with the testimonies and autorities of the auncient fathers againste all suche errors and heresies as the Papistes haue brought into the Churche, aboute the doctrine of the Sacrament of the body and bloud of Christ. First published in the folio edition.

* 58. The Monstruous Marchandise of the Romish Bishops whereunto is added the judgement of certen learned men concerninge Rome and the state thereof, and what is to be thought of the Bishop of Rome, his authoritye and primacye. First published in the folio edition. The latter part of this treatise is the " old book made by Becon entitled *Reports of Certain Men* " to which Strype refers, see *Cranmer*, p. 244 and pp. 795-799, App. XXXIX.

* 59. The relickes of Rome. *J. Day : London* [1560 ?]. 8vo. [*STC* 1754].
    59a. The Reliques of Rome, contayning all such matters of Religion, as have in times past bene brought into the Church by the Pope and his adherentes : faithfully gathered out of the most faithful writers of Chronicles and Histories, and now newly both diligently corrected and greatly augmented, to the singuler profit of the Readers, by Thomas Becon, 1563. Preface dated 6th June, 1563. [This is no doubt the edition mentioned by Lowndes, *op. cit.*, i, p. 143 ; he gives as the date, 1553, which is certainly a mistake].

* 60. The Diuersitie betweene God's worde and Mannes inuentions. First published in the folio edition. A free version of Francois Lambert's Antithesis verbi dei & inventorū hominum.
    60a. The Diversity between God's Word and Man's Invention, *etc.* Tercentenary Tracts ; or Tracts written by British Reformers 1835. 12mo.

* 61. The Actes of Christe & of Antichrist, concerning both their life and doctrine. First published in the folio edition.
    61a. another edition. The Actes of Christe and of Antichriste, concernyng bothe their life and doctrines : diligently gathered and now taken out of his workes by T. Becon. *Ihon Daie : London*, 1577. 8vo.

* 62. Christes Chronicle, contayning brieflye in a most goodly and pleasaunt order whatsoever is written at large in the Gospels of the foure Euangelistes. First published in the folio edition.

* 63. The Summarie of the New Testament orderly and briefly declaryng the contentes of every Chapiter thorow out the whole Boke. First published in the folio edition.

* 64. The Demandes of holy Scripture with answers to the same, wherein are defined and declared the chiefe and principal points of Christian doctrine : verye profitable for the right understanding of the holy Scriptures. First published in the folio edition. Preface dated 1st September, 1563.
    64a. another edition. The Demaundes of Holy Scripture, with answeres to the same, wherein are defined and declared the cheefe and principall poyntes of Christian doctrine, *etc.*, *Iohn Day : London.* 1577. 8vo.

* 65. The Glorious triumphe of Gods most blessed word. First published in the folio edition. Preface dated 6th October, 1563.

* 66. The prayse of Death, set forth in a dialoge betwene man and Reason. First published in the folio edition.

§ 67. Letter to Archbishop Parker. Corpus Christi College, Cambridge, MSS—M. R. James's Catalogue, item 302 in MS 114.

68. The workes of Thomas Becon, which he hath hytherto made and published, with diuerse other newe Bookes added to the same, heretofore neuer set forth in print diuided into thre tomes or parts diligently perused, corrected, and amended : and now finished this present of our Lord, 1564. 3 vols, folio. *Iohn Day* : *London* 1560, 1563, and 1564.

    68a. The Works of Thomas Becon, edited for the Parker Society by the Rev. John Ayre, M.A.

        Vol. I.   Early Works, *Cambridge*, 1843.

        Vol. II.   Catechism and other pieces, *Cambridge*, 1844.

        Vol. III.   Prayers and other pieces, *Cambridge*, 1844.

    [From this edition the following are omitted : Nos. 1, 10-12, 15, 17, 19-21, 23, 25, 30, 35-36, 41, 43-52, 54, 58-59, 65-66, and 69. No. 67 is printed in the Preface.]

§ 69. A New Postil Conteinyng most Godly and learned sermons upon all the Sonday Gospelles, that be redde in the Church throwout the yeare : lately set foorth unto the great profite not onely of al Curates, and spirituall Ministers, but also of all other godly & Faythfull Readers. 2 vols. 4to. *Thomas Marshe* : *London*, 1566. [*STC* 1736].

    69a. another edition, as above, 1567. 4to. [*STC* 1737].

    69b. Faith in Christ ; the Gospel for Whit-Monday, from Postils by Thomas Becon, in The Testimony of the Reformers, by the Rev. E. Bickersteth, *London*, 1836.

B. WORKS ATTRIBUTED TO BECON

1. Christian Prayers and Godly Meditations upon the Epistle of St. Paul to the Romans, attributed to Becon by Tanner, p. 86, who describes it : " ex Italico. Pr. ded. magistro T. M. ' Of how great efficacy virtue.' dat. Shenae, 12 Febr. MDL.; Lond. MDLXIX. 24to." This cannot be traced, and is not listed in *STC*.

2. English verses prefixed to The eyght tragedie of Seneca : Agamemnon. *Tr.* John Studley. *T. Colwell*, 1566, 8vo. [*STC* 22222]. The poem is signed T.B., but internal evidence is against authorship by Becon.

3. At the end of the translation of the Psalms included in the " Bishops' Bible " published in 1572 occur the initials T.B. which, says Strype, " perhaps designate Thomas Becon." (*Parker*, ii, p. 222.) There is no supporting evidence for this attribution.

C. ANTHOLOGIES, ETC.

1. Prayers, by Thomas Becon (Selections from the Writings of the Reformers and Fathers of the Church of England, No. 6), *S.P.C.K. London*, 1836, 12mo. A reprint of various prayers.

2. The Writings of the Rev. Thomas Becon, *R.T.S.*: *London* [? 1830]. Selections from Becon's works ; 12mo.

3. Becon's Golden Saying [a religious tract]. *J. Groom* : *Birmingham* [? 1855], 8vo.

II

WORKS QUOTED OR MENTIONED IN THE COURSE OF THIS STUDY

In every case the edition given is that to which reference has been made.

AMES, JOSEPH : *Typographical Antiquities*, ed. Dibdin, London, 1819.

ARBER, E.: *Transcript of the Registers of the Company of Stationers*, London, 1875.

(ed.)—*A Brief Discourse of the Troubles at Frankfort*, London, 1908.

BALE, JOHN : *Scriptorum Illustrium maioris Britanniae . . . Catalogus*, Basle, 1557.

Index Britanniae Scriptorum, ed. R. L. Poole and M. Bateson, Oxford, 1902.

BENNET, E. K.: *The College of St. John the Evangelist of Rushworth—Norfolk Archaeology*, vol. x, pt. 1 (1884) and vol. x, pt. 3 (1887).

BENSON, ARTHUR CHRISTOPHER : *The Life of Edward White Benson*, 2 vols. London, 1899.

BRADFORD, JOHN : *The Writings of. . . . Sermons, Meditations, Examinations, &c. (PS)*, Cambridge, 1848.

The Writings of. . . . Letters, Treatises, Remains (PS), Cambridge, 1853.

BRETT, JOHN : *Narrative of the Pursuit of English Refugees in Germany under Q. Mary*, ed. I. S. Leadam, *R.H.S. Trans.* New Series, vol. xi, 1897.

BRIGHTMAN, F. E.: *The English Rite*, 2 vols. London, 1915.

BROOK, BENJAMIN : *The Lives of the Puritans*, 3 vols. London, 1813.

BULLINGER, HENRY : *The Decades (PS)*, 4 vols. Cambridge, 1849-1852.

BURNET, GILBERT : *The History of the Reformation of the Church of England*, ed. N. Pocock, 7 vols. Oxford, 1865.

CALVIN, JOHN : *Ioannis Calvini . . . Opera Omnia*, 9 vols. Amstelodami, 1672.

CARDWELL, EDWARD : *Synodalia*, 2 vols. Oxford, 1842.

CHURTON, E.: *Life of Alexander Nowell*, Oxford, 1809.

COLLIGAN, J. HAY : *The Honourable William Whittingham of Chester*, Chester and London, 1934.

CONSTANT, G.: *The Reformation in England. II. Introduction of the Reformation into England. Edward VI (1547-1553).* Trans. by E. I. Watkin, London, 1942, from the French : *La Reforme En Angleterre II, L'Introduction De La Reforme En Angleterre. Edouard VI*, 1547-1553, Paris, 1939.

COOPER, CHARLES HENRY, and COOPER, THOMPSON : *Athenae Cantabrigienses*, vol. I., Cambridge, 1858.

CRANMER, THOMAS : *Writings and Disputations of . . . relative to the . . . Lord's Supper (PS)*, Cambridge, 1844.

Miscellaneous Writings and Letters of. . . . (PS), Cambridge, 1846.

DEMAUS, ROBERT : *Hugh Latimer*, London, 1904.

Dictionary of National Biography

DIX, GREGORY : *Dixit Cranmer et non Timuit*—articles in the *Church Quarterly Review.* Jan.-March, and April-June, 1948.

DIXON, RICHARD WATSON : *History of the Church of England*, vols. I-IV, London, 1878-1891.

EADIE, JOHN : *The English Bible*, 2 vols. London, 1876.

ELLIS, H.: *The History and Antiquities of the Parish of Shoreditch and Liberty of Norton Folgate in the suburbs of London*, London, 1798.

English Historical Review, vol. xix (1904).

FOSTER, J.: *Alumni Oxonienses* (early series), Oxford, 1891.

FOXE, JOHN : *The Acts and Monuments of. . . .*, ed. Josiah Pratt, 8 vols· London, 1870.
Narratives of the Reformation, ed. J. G. Nichols (Camden Society), 1859.

FROUDE, JAMES ANTHONY : *History of England*, 12 vols. London, n.d.

FULKE, WILLIAM : *A Defence of the . . . translations of the Holy Scriptures . . . (PS)*, Cambridge, 1843.
Answers to Stapleton, Martiall, and Sanders *(PS)*, Cambridge, 1848.

GARRETT, CHRISTINA HALLOWELL : *The Marian Exiles*, Cambridge, 1938.

GEE, HENRY : *The Elizabethan Clergy and the Settlement of Religion*, 1558-1564, Oxford, 1898.

GEE, HENRY, and HARDY, WILLIAM JOHN : *Documents Illustrative of English Church History*, London, 1910.

GLOVER, S.: *History of the County of Derby*, ed. T. Noble, Derby, 1829.

HAWEIS, J. O. W.: *Sketches of the Reformation*, London, 1844.

HENNESSY, G.: *Novum Repertorium Ecclesiasticum Parochiale Londinense*, London, 1898.

HOLLAND : *Heroologia Anglica*, 1620.

Homilies: *Certain Sermons or Homilies appointed to be read in Churches . . .*, London, 1843 (S.P.C.K. edition).

HOOPER, JOHN : *Early Writings of . . . (PS)*, Cambridge, 1843.

HOPF, CONSTANTIN : *Martin Bucer and the English Reformation*, Oxford, 1946.

HOW, F. D.: *Archbishop Maclagan*, London, 1911.

HUTCHINSON, ROGER : *The Works of . . . (PS)*, Cambridge, 1842.

JACOBS, HENRY EYSTER : *The Lutheran Movement in England. . . .* Philadelphia, 1890.
The Lutheran Element in Early English Catechisms—article in *The Lutheran Church Review*, No. 3, July, 1888.

JESSOP, A.: *Visitations of the Diocese of Norwich A.D.* 1492-1552, Camden Society xliii (NS), 1888.

JONSON, BEN : *Works*, ed. Gifford, 9 vols. London, 1875.

KENNEDY, W. M.: *The " Interpretations " of the Bishops* (Alcuin Club Tracts VIII), London, 1908.

KNOX, JOHN : *The Works of . . .*, ed. David Laing, vols. III (1854) and IV (1855), Edinburgh.

LATIMER, HUGH : *Sermons (PS)*, Cambridge, 1844.
Sermons and Remains (PS), Cambridge, 1845.

LEADAM, I. S.: see BRETT.

LE NEVE, J.: *Fasti Ecclesiae Anglicanae*, ed. Sir T. D. Hardy, Oxford, 1854, 3 vols.

Letters and Papers, Henry VIII, Foreign and Domestic.

LINDSAY, THOMAS M.: *A History of the Reformation*, 2 vols. Edinburgh, 1906-1907.

Liturgies : *The two Liturgies . . . with other Documents . . . King Edward VI* (PS), Cambridge, 1844.
Liturgies and Occasional Forms of Prayer . . . Queen Elizabeth (PS), Cambridge, 1847.

LLOYD, CHARLES : *Formularies of Faith put forth by Authority during the reign of Henry VIII*, ed. by, Oxford, 1825.

LORIMER, PETER : *John Knox and the Church of England*, London, 1875.

LOWNDES, W. T.: *The Bibliographer's Manual*, London, 1857.

LUPTON, DONALD : *The History of the Moderne Protestant Divines*, London, 1637.

MACHYN, HENRY : *Diary*, Camden Society, London, 1848.

MAITLAND, S. R.: *Essays on . . . the Reformation in England*, London, 1849.

MARSTON, JOHN : *Works*, ed. Bullen, London, 1887.

MAYCOCK, A. L.: *Nicholas Ferrar of Little Gidding*, London, 1938.

MULLINGER, JAMES BASS : *The University of Cambridge*, Cambridge, 1873, 2 vols.

NEWCOURT, RICHARD : *Repertorium Ecclesiasticum Parochiale Londonense*, London, 1708.

NICHOL : *The County of Leicester*, London, 1795.

Original Letters Relative to the English Reformation . . . 2 vols. (PS), Cambridge, 1846-1847.

PARKER, MATTHEW : *Correspondence of . . .* (PS), Cambridge, 1853.
Registrum Matthei Parker Dioc : *Cant* : 1559-1575 (Canterbury and York Society), Oxford, 1928-1933.

POLLARD, A. F.: *The History of England from the accession of Edward VI to the death of Elizabeth* (Political History of England, vol. VI), London, 1919.

POLLARD AND REDGRAVE : *Short Title Catalogue of English Books*, 1475-1640, London, 1926.

REDSTONE, V. B.: *Chapels, Chantries, and Gilds in Suffolk*, article in *Suffolk Inst. of Archaeology and Natural History*, vol. xii (1), 1904.

Reformatio Legum Ecclesiasticarum, ed. Edward Cardwell, Oxford, 1850.

RICHARDSON, CYRIL C.: *Zwingli and Cranmer on the Eucharist*, Evanston, 1949.

RIDLEY, NICHOLAS : *The Works of . . .* (PS), Cambridge, 1841.

RITSON : *Bibliographia Poetica*, London, 1802.

SANDYS, EDWIN : *Sermons* (PS), Cambridge, 1841.

SELWYN, EDWARD GORDON : *The First Epistle of St. Peter*, London, 1946.

SMITH, RICHARD : *Confutatio eorum, quae Philippus Melanchthon obijcit contra Missae sacrificium propitiatorium*, Louvaine, 1562.

SMYTH, C. H.: *Cranmer and the Reformation under Edward VI*, Cambridge, 1924.

SPEARING, E. M.: *Studley's Translations of Seneca's Agamemnon and Medea*, ed. from the octavos of 1566, Louvain, 1913.

State Papers, Edward VI, vol. x, pt. ii.

STERRY, WASEY : *Eton College Register*, Eton, 1943.

STONE, DARWELL : *A History of the Doctrine of the Holy Eucharist*, 2 vols., London, 1909.

STRYPE, JOHN : *Annals of the Reformation* . . ., 3 vols. 6 pts. Oxford, 1824.
   . . . *The Life and Acts of* . . . *John Aylmer* . . . Oxford, 1821.
Memorials of . . . *Thomas Cranmer* . . ., 2 vols., Oxford, 1840.
Ecclesiastical Memorials . . ., 3 vols., 6 pts. Oxford, 1822.
   . . . *the Life and Acts of* . . . *Edmund Grindal*. . . . Oxford, 1821.
The Life and Acts of Matthew Parker . . ., 3 vols., Oxford, 1821.

SYKES, NORMAN : *The Crisis of the Reformation*, London, 1946.

TANNER, THOMAS : *Bibliotheca Britannico-Hibernia*, London, 1748.

TAWNEY, R. H.: *Religion and the rise of Capitalism*, London, 1926.

TIMMS, G. B.: *Dixit Cranmer*—articles in the *Church Quarterly Review*, Jan.-March and April-June, 1947.

Troubles—A Brieff discours off the troubles begonne at Franckford in Germany Anno Domini 1554 . . ., 1575, reprinted, London, 1846.

TYNDALE, WILLIAM : *Doctrinal Treatises* . . . (*PS*), Cambridge, 1848.

VENN, JOHN and J. A.: *Alumni Cantabrigienses*, Cambridge, 1922.

WHITGIFT, JOHN : *The Works of* . . . (*PS*), 3 vols. Cambridge, 1851-1853.

WODDERSPOON, J.: *Memorials of Ipswich*, Ipswich and London, 1850.

WRIOTHESLEY, C.: *Chronicle*, 2 vols. Camden Society, London, 1875.   89

INDEX

Abell, John, 79.
Alexandre, Pierre, 79.
Alsop, John, 49.
Alsop, Thomas, 49 n.1.
Alvey, Richard, 6.
Anne of Cleves, 55.
Aylmer, John, 52.

Bale, John, 6, 80, 81, 82.
Barnesdale, Thomas, 11, 12 n.2.
Basil, Theodore—see Becon, Thomas.
Beaseley, Richard, 56 n.1.
Becon, Basil I, 90, 91, 125.
Becon, Basil II, 125, 126-127, 134.
Becon, Christophile, 91, 125.
Becon, Elizabeth (dau. of Basil II), 126.
Becon, Elizabeth (dau. of Theodore II), 126.
Becon, John, xv, 1.
Becon, John (son of Basil II), 127.
Becon, Rachel, 91, 125.
Becon, Rachel (dau. of Basil II), 126.
Becon, Theodore I, 91, 125, 132.
Becon, Theodore II, 2 n.5, 125, 126.
Becon, Theodore (son of Basil II), 127.
Becon (Beacon, Beaton, Bacon, Bekon), Thomas, Birth and childhood, 1, 130-131; life at Cambridge, 2-7; hears Latimer preach, 3; his

reminiscences of Stafford, 5; his academical career, 131-132; admitted B.A., 6, 130; his ordination, 8, 132-134; Fellow of Rushworth College, 7-12; named in connexion with the appointment of a priest to the chantry of St. Thomas in the church of St. Lawrence, Ipswich, 13-14; apprehended for preaching in Norfolk and Suffolk and made to recant, 15-17; his first recantation, 17, 32; retires into Kent and adopts the pseudonym Theodore Basil, 18; his writings during 1541-1543, 19-29; taken and made to recant the second time, 30-31; his second recantation, 31-32; he journeys to Norfolk and thence to the Peak, 49; — to Staffordshire, 50; — to Warwickshire, 51; — to Leicestershire, 52; his books condemned, 52-53; appointed one of the six Canterbury Preachers, 55; appointed a licensed preacher, 56; presented to the Rectory of St. Stephen, Walbrook, 57; committed to the Tower, 77; released, 78; escapes to the Continent, 79; in exile at Strasbourg, 84-85; goes to Frankfort, 85; appointed 'Minister' there, 87; goes to Marburg, 90; returns to

England, 90-91 ; made Canon of Canterbury, 92 ; — Rector of Buckland, 93 ; — Vicar of Christ Church, Newgate, 93 ; — Vicar of Sturry, 93 ; reinstated in the Rectory of St. Stephen, Walbrook, which he later resigns, 93 ; made Rector of St. Dionys Backchurch, 93 ; his preaching, 94 ; clerical Visitor for south-east England, 94-95 ; acts on behalf of the Archbishop of Canterbury, 95 ; Visitor of Eastbridge Hospital, Canterbury, 95 ; his certificate furnished to Parker, 96 ; prepares a collected edition of his works, 96-97 ; his controversy with Dr. Richard Smith, 98 ; his part in the proceedings of the Convocation of 1562-3, 100-101 ; at first refuses, but later conforms to Grindal's regulations concerning habits, 102 ; his death, 104.

His doctrine of the Church, 105-106 ; — of the Sacraments, 106-107 ; — of baptism, 107 ; — of the Eucharist, 108-111 ; — of marriage, 111-115.

His writings — their purpose and characteristics, 115-116 ; his devotional works, 116-117 ; the historical importance of his works, 117 ; his significance as a reformer, 117-119.

As a writer, 120-123 ; popular elements in his works, 121-123 ; his verse, 124.

His family and their descendants, 124-127.

Becon, Thomas (son of Basil II), 127.
Bernard, Thomas, 6.
Beswick (Berwick), William, 127.
Bilney, Thomas, 2, 3.
Bonner, Edmund, 15, 26.
Bourne, Gilbert, 77.
Bradford, John, 77.
Brett, John, 89
Bucer, Martin, 110.
Buckenham, Robert, 4 n.4.
Bullinger, Henry, 22.

Calvin, John, 75, 76, 87, 97.
Carew, Peter, 79.
Cecil, Thomas, 69.
Cecil, William, 79, 92-94.
Chambers, Richard, 85.
Cheke, John, 6, 79.
Cheney, Richard, 132.
Coale, Anne, 126.
Cooke, Anthony, 79.
Coverdale, Myles, 22, 23.
Cox, Richard, 78, 84-89, 118.
Cranmer, Thomas, 5-6, 18, 55, 57, 70, 76, 78, 88, 106, 110-111, 118, 137.
Crawford, James, 12-14.
Croftes, John, 11, 12 n.2.
Crome, Edward, 79.
Cromwell, Thomas, 12-13, 25.

Daundy, Edmund, 12-14.
Day, John, 96.

Erasmus, Desiderius, 3.

Feilding, Basil, 51 n.2.
Fisher, William, 11, 12 n.2.
Foxe, John, xiii, 4, 15-17, 26, 47, 77.

Gardiner, Stephen, 79, 81.
Gilby, Anthony, 6.

Gilpin, Bernard, 60.
Glover, John, 51.
Gonvile, Edmund, 9.
Goodman, Christopher, 83.
Gough, John, 23.
Grindal, Edmund, 85, 99, 102, 118-119.

Hanson, Edward, 11, 12.
Haynes, Simon, 57.
Henry VIII, King, 3, 5, 23-24, 26-27.
Heton, Thomas, 79.
Hooper, John, 51 n.1, 59, 76 n.1, 117.
Horne, Robert, 85
Horne, Thomas, 11, 12 n.2.
Hutchinson, Roger, 71.

Jonson, Ben, 68.
Joseph, John, 56 n.1.

Kitchen, Anthony, 132.
Knox, John, 69-71, 76, 83-84, 86-87, 118.

Lambert, Francois, 99.
Laski, John, 71, 73.
Latimer, Hugh, 3-5, 51, 54, 78, 117-118, 121.
Locke, Robert, 11, 12 n.2.
Luther, Martin, 136-137.

Machyn, Henry, 94.
Mary, Queen, 6, 81, 83.
Mayler, John, 23, 30 n.2.
Merbeck, John, 30.
Moore, Thomas, 99.
Morison, Richard, 79.

Neville, Thomas, 19.
Northumberland, John Dudley, Duke of, 59 n.1.

Olde, John, 50-51, 54.

Parker, Matthew, 66 n.3, 94, 102.
Pecocke, Thomas, 14 n.1.
Philip, Landgrave of Hesse, 89.
Pierpount, George, 19.
Pimpe, Reginald, 14.
Pole, Reginald, 20, 95.
Ponet, John, 6, 59 n.1, 79-81, 83, 85, 137.
Porter, John, 26.

Redman, John, 57-58.
Ridley, Lancelot, 56 n.1.
Ridley, Nicholas, 48, 56 n.1, 65 n.3, 78-79.
Rogers, John, 79.
Roydon, Margaret, 14.
Roydon, Thomas, 14.

Sampson, Thomas, 79-80.
Sandys, Edwin, 48, 78-80.
Saunders, Lawrence, 79.
Scott, Mary, 14.
Scott, Richard, 14.
Seymour, Lady Jane, 54.
Singleton, Robert, 30-32.
Smith, Richard, 98, 132 n.1.
Smythe, Dorcas, 126.
Somerset, Anne, Duchess of, 54.
Somerset, Edward, Duke of, 6, 54-55, 61.
Stafford, George, 5, 118.
Studley, 123.

Taylor, John, 57-58, 137.
Tonge, Roger, 57.
Traheron, Bartholomew, 83.
Turner, Richard, 56 n.1.
Turner, William, 6, 123.
Tyndale, William, 113.

Underwood, John, 8.

Vermigli, Peter Martyr, 79.
Veron, John, 77, 79.

Warham, William, 4 n.3.
Watson, Robert, 66 n.3.
Wentworth, Richard, 14.
Wentworth, Thomas, Lord, 6, 13-14, 26, 54, 134.
Wharton, Thomas, 3.
Whetnall, George, 20.
Whetnall, Margaret, 14.
Whetnall, Thomas, 20.
Whittingham, William, 84, 102, 118.

William of Hesse, 90.
Willington, Godith, 51 n.2.
Wingfield, Lady Anne, 10.
Wisdom, Robert, 6, 15-16, 30-31, 46-47, 50.
Wotton, Thomas, 112.
Wrothe, Thomas, 79.
Wyatt, Thomas, 20-21, 28.
Wyndham, George, 11, 12 n.2.

Zwingli, Ulrich, 106, 110-111.